About This Issue

Fifteen years ago we published the first of four issues on the history of African Americans, "The Black Catholic Experience." We are grateful to have been the publisher of the proceedings of the 1987 National Black Catholic Congress, "The Black Catholic Community." New explorations of several spheres of local history were featured in "African Americans and their Church." Though we have included articles on Black Catholic history in other issues, this publication is our first foray into liturgical studies. We are especially pleased to bring together scholars identified with African American liturgical renewal to mark our entrance into a new area for us and to underscore our commitment to African American Catholic studies. We are also grateful to Father Clarence-Rufus J. Rivers for his autobiographical reflection that so aptly connects the themes of this issue and contributes meaning to the historical experiences of African American Catholics during the critical periods of the past fifty years. M. Shawn Copeland is professor of theology at Marquette University in Milwaukee, Wisconsin. Cyprian Davis, O.S.B. is professor of history and archivist at St. Mienard Archabbey and Seminary in St. Mienard, Indiana. Diana L. Hayes, theologian and attorney, is associate professor of theology at Georgetown University. Tammy Lynn Kernodle is an assistant professor of musicology at Miami University of Ohio in Oxford, Ohio. Eva Marie Lumas, O.S.F. is assistant professor of faith and culture and Mary E. McGann, R.S.C.J. is assistant professor of music and liturgy at the Franciscan School of Theology in Berkeley, California. Clarence-Rufus J. Rivers, a priest of the Archdiocese of Cincinnati, is the founder and director of Stimuli, Inc. He is committed to establishing the Lion of Judah Institute, a college of apprenticeship, to graduate not only scholars but especially worship professionals, liturgical practitioners, and worship impresarios. Cyprian L. Rowe, former director of the National Office for Black Catholics and professor of social work at the Johns Hopkins University, has been involved in several ministries, including African American liturgical renewal. His article should be viewed as a poem in progress.

We welcome William Dinges as an associate editor of our journal. Professor Dinges is on the faculty of the department of religion and religious education at the Catholic University of America in Washington, D.C.

CJK

African American Spirituality: Scenes, Stories, and Meanings

Cyprian L. Rowe

Part I

These images endure:

Scene One
My mother, even into her old age, kneeling by her bed every night and summing up the gratitude and the glory of her day (whether it had been good or bad in the minds of others); it had been the glory of her day and for that she had thanked her God.

Scene Two
My mother prostrating, her head bent to the floor and wailing whenever one who was dear passed on. Even if I tried to embrace her before she went to the floor, she resisted my arms and responded to the necessity of her rite.

And at the last: my leaning over her and telling her just to give herself to Jesus and her nodding that she always had.

Part II

Sitting in the Ahenfie (palace of the Chief/King) in Dompim-Pepesa hearing the wailing of the women giving vent to the pain of the people when one had gone before. It is the recognition that death exists and there is a pain of loss; but, too, that the eternal always has dominion and one who has gone has gone ahead to wait for us all and can upon occasion, in ways that we feel and know, somehow, speak to us and guide.

African spirituality and its "children" are spiritualities of the immediate, of the here and the now and the always, of the eternal and the eternal which is ever in the NOW. One walks in the Ocean of God. One walks knowing that God is God and God is love and God is Goodness and Mercy and Justice and God is rhythm and music and feasting and sacrifice and sharing the roasted lamb among all of the people after having given back to the Father-Mother all that which belongs to the Divine.

It was nothing that African people learned, not like ABCs. It was felt in Adamic beginnings. But it can be deepened. It was, if one inquired in a Western way, "what was known because it was known, was there because it was/is there," like Bernadette's Lady at Lourdes, with some sense of amazement, asking the others: "Don't you see her?"

African American spirituality has at its viscera a sense of passion for the Other, the reality of the Other because human beings are made fully human only in the community of persons who are being drawn together and together drawn to the CENTER OF ALL BEING, . . . which ever as we walk their earth is always with us and in us and through us TOGETHER!

It is a sense of the OTHER as the mirror of the self, insofar as entitlement goes. It is a sense of the other as the immediate and intimate source of my sanctification/growth into divinity IN THE NOW MOMENT. It is a knowing that the Other, whether he/she does me well or ill, is constantly calling me to a place at which the Lord is speaking higher and deeper TRUTH.

Another Image from My Past

I was a scholastic. In our Brotherhood, this was our college. At the end of supper one evening, the superior stood up and began his announcements by stating: "This might be a n——r in the woodpile but . . ." The entire dining room erupted in laughter. Over a hundred scholastics and faculty erupted in laughter! Burst into riotous laughter and since they had, in effect, been given permission to use that word that was always anathema in my home, the word assaulted me hundreds of times that night. Hurtful beyond measure it seemed when the Chinese Brothers and Spanish Brothers wrapped their foreign tongues around the word. That happened in 1954, over forty-five years ago. And yet, it happens still, for memories are insistent where there is insufficient healing. And yet over these years, the superior who used this totally ignorant term has been an advocate for me in every way and, I am sure, was ignorant even back then. But knives and sticks have no eyes and no hands. They land where the striker aims them. But still. I and we have endured and in the Spirit, we know that all, ultimately, is good if we say "yeas" to the task of transformation.

Indeed, neither Martin nor Malcolm yearned for death. Neither did those Africans, women and men to be slaves, who jumped into eternal sea by way of the Atlantic and Indian Oceans.

African American spirituality is a spirituality of transformative power, the core of a world that is worth dying for because ultimate life is always victorious over all forms of death and dying. That Martin and Malcolm, "that all that train seized hold of the moment, of the blood"; to be salvific like Christ is part of that spirituality that strives ever to show the heaven that is ever present in the now.

African American Spirit
Knows
That even as you murder
The Dreamers
They and the Dream
Shall mount up like
Signal fires
On the mountaintop
And all shall see the Light
And read the Truth
And follow in the Way. . .

And so I must see the sin of his ignorance as a grace that calls me continually TO wholeness—a wholeness that in its insistence on the ultimate spirit of life rises above all that is/was meant to hold it down.

These are not my thoughts.

These are the thoughts of my Mother and of my mothers and fathers and of all those who have in LIFE called me into FULLNESS. It is a profound sense that I must rest in my own heart and trust. It is a sense that all will happen that is meant to happen and that gives me a reality that is always what it should be according to what I need here and now and into an eternity that is, ever, implicit in the here and in the now.

Let Me End as I Began

Scenes: Dr. Martin Luther King's Life and One from My Mother's Dying:
Both from the Same Spirit
Early on, not too long after the beginning of the Holy War for Freedom for all, Martin came to Harlem. During a talk there, a Black woman, calling him a Communist, walked up to him and plunged a knitting needle into his side, just missing his heart. While he knew how close he had been to death, he feared neither death nor those who could bring it as long as the Lord was calling him to this work.

When it was clear to me that Mother was going to go to the Lord, that the call was irrevocable, I leaned over and whispered into her ear, "Mother, just give yourself to Jesus." And Mother responded, "I already have."

Finally Final
I always fear that my life, i.e., my entering the religious life at the age of fifteen and living always in and/or near that environment, made me want to share thoughts from two others who have fought the daily fight that I am not sure I understand in the same way. So I asked two friends to share their thoughts. One, Mr. Robert Abrams, has

pursued a vision for his entire adult life—that vision being the sharing of wholesome food with poor people, making a number of fruits and vegetables available at the unchanging price of two pounds for a quarter. The second piece is by a Mr. James Brightful, who calls his piece "Moved by the Holy Ghost."

A Porlina Story:

Mrs. Chestnut all in white, her spotless white tea cup, and her one tea bag used over and over and over again, by Robert John Abrams

The other day Brother Cyprian asked me: What do you understand Black Spirituality is? And that is right! Brother Cyprian asked a question and gave the answer. Black Spirituality is!

Black Spirituality is real! You sing! You shout! You moan! You run! You just sit still and raise your hand; you cry you know weeping may endure for the night but you know joy comes in the morning you know He may not come when you want Him but He's always right on time you know you can call Him up anytime you want because you have a telephone in your bosom you feel sometimes like a motherless child a long way from home but you know soon early in the morning you're going home you know that all day all night the angels keep watch over you and you know this joy you have the world didn't give it to you, you know when it gets inside you you look at your hands and they're new you look at your feet and they're new too it's just like fire! Fi-yah! Shut up in your veins and you just start runnin' runnin' for Jesus and you're not tired yet!

Black Spirituality is. Black Spirituality is real.

When I was a little boy in the depression time when Pop worked three and four jobs, and washed and ironed his own clothes, mended his own shoes, walked ten and twelve miles to work so Mom could be always with the four children, so that we would have a house with a garden for Mom: Pop and Mom rented the top, third-floor room to a rollypolly chestnut brown, sparkling bright eyed, always smiling, always dressed in immaculately white, white dress: Mrs. Chestnut.

Mrs. Chestnut was a Holy Roller and Mrs. Chestnut did day's work for a fat white doctor way out on City Line. Mrs. Chestnut was the fat white doctor's doctor. And so even when he did not have money enough to pay, Mrs. Chestnut would come down every morning to the kitchen at 8 a.m. in her white white oh so white dress, carrying on a tray covered by a white, white oh so white napkin, a white white shining white tea cup. And on the tray wrapped in another white napkin lay a single tea bag that Mrs. Chestnut used over and over and over because she did not have money enough to buy more tea because the little money she had she divided in tithes for the Church and the rest was divided between a tiny loaf of bread and carfare to go to do day's work for the fat white doctor.

Mrs. Chestnut would come into the kitchen, place the tray on the table, lift the white napkin from the tray, fold it neatly and place it on the tray, lift the spotless white tea cup and hold it in her cupped hands, close her eyes and quietly say: Thank you, Lord. Place the cup on the table, go to the stove and place a sauce pan with water on the burner, and, when the water was hot, pour it into the spotless white tea cup, unfold the napkin that held the one tea bag, lift the tea bag gently and place it in the upturned palm of her right hand and lift both of her hands up and with eyes looking up to heaven say quietly: Thank you, Lord. Then Mrs. Chestnut would gently dip the tea bag once, twice, a third time into the steaming water, lift it out and with her silver spoon carefully press the water out of the bag into the saucer of the tea cup, place the tea bag back into the napkin, fold it over then fold her hands, bow her head, and say: Thank you, Lord.

Black Spirituality is. Black Spirituality is real. Black Spirituality is Mrs. Chestnut all in white, her spotless white tea cup, and her one tea bag used over and over and over again.

Moved by the Holy Ghost, by James Brightfield

Black Spirituality, what does that mean to me? That is a rather difficult question to answer. I grew up living outside the Black religious community. As a child my religious development was European and not African based.

I was a minority within the Roman Catholic faith. I attended church and school in a parish where I was recognized as an individual with a history and/or culture different of those of my friends. The skin color was different, the hair was different, but my spiritual needs were not treated as different.

God was portrayed as White, so was Christ. The dogma was European, the laws were enforced by a European White man in Rome. The sermons were preached by white men, the lessons taught by White women. Looking back at it now my religious development and my African ancestry were in no way related to one another. I was a Black child with the soul of a white child.

Not until I grew older did I realize Black people in many cases worshiped differently, were taught differently. So much of the religion they practiced was infused with the culture of their motherland. Their religion and their racial identity were in many cases wedded. They belonged to a church that fought for their civil rights; they were part of a community that reached back across the Atlantic to Africa. They sang and shouted with the rhythms of a truly jubilant people. They were a people who knew the pains of bondage and slavery, but now they were free.

As a child I attended church every Sunday, St. Marks, a church named for a long-dead White man. The church, a grand and ornate palace which accommodated hundreds, was rarely full except on major holy days. I sat in pious solitude for one hour listening to a service conducted for the most part in a European language long out of popular use, which I could not comprehend. The readings were of a people whom I could not relate to. The hymns were sedate lyrics of reverence and adoration. I left the church no more richer or enlightened than when I entered.

Just up the hill was Grace A.M.E. Church, a church named for a blessing that those in attendance were looking forward to having showered upon them. The church, a small, rather simple structure, appeared always to be at full to overflowing attendance. On those hot summer days the doors had to be left open in order to bring a breeze into the church. The music rose up out of the church like joyous celebration and an occasional shout out could also be heard from the street. One could not help be impressed by the exit of churchgoers who were in their words, "moved by the Holy Ghost."

As an adult I realized how deprived I was of so much; I grew disappointed and disenchanted with the Church itself. As years passed the Catholic Church realized that it was not fulfilling the needs of its African American congregations. It has brought about changes that only now address the needs of its disenfranchised people. I now attend a Catholic Church after years away, and I do feel a spirit rise up inside of me that was never there before. I do not know if it is because we have a Black priest, the songs are now more gospel tempered, and there are the occasional shout out or hand clap for God. The one thing I do appreciate most is that I think at least at the Church of the Nativity, its parishioners are now moved by the Holy Ghost.

Some Reflections on African American Catholic Spirituality

Cyprian Davis, O.S.B.

Daniel Rudd, journalist, lecturer, polemicist, convinced Catholic, and newspaper editor, was directly responsible for the convening of the first Black Catholic Lay Congress in 1889. In the columns of his newspaper, the *American Catholic Tribune,* Rudd talked about the importance of Black Catholics coming together to know each other and to exchange ideas. He saw them as uniting among themselves, and, as he put it, "taking up the cause of the race." Expressing it in another way, he wrote: "Colored Catholics should step forward and convince their people, that none love them better; none [are] more anxious for their welfare; none more ready to advance their cause than their brethren of the Catholic Church."[1] Rudd was responding to the notion that "[the] Colored Catholic must at times, feel that his Colored brethren look upon him as an alien"; in other words, one who did not fit into the African American world.

In response to this notion, Rudd suggested that the African American Catholic community had what one might call "a mission." He defined this mission in this way: "The Catholics of the Colored race should be the leaven, which would raise up their people not only in the eye of God but before men." Later in the article, he referred to Black Catholics in this country as deliberating together and "uniting on a course of action, behind which would stand the majestic Church of Christ, they must inevitably become . . . the bearer of their race." Typically, Rudd unconsciously had lapsed into the language of Scripture. This leaven or yeast is from the parable of the woman preparing to bake bread: "To what shall I compare the kingdom of God? It is like yeast that a woman took and mixed in with three measures of wheat flour until the whole batch of dough was leavened."[2] The number of Black Catholics might be small, but, like the Kingdom, they can transform the entire Black American community.

---

1. *American Catholic Tribune,* 4 May 1888.
2. Lk 13:21; also Mt 13:33.

The notion of being "bearers of the race" suggests Paul's Letter to the Galatians:

> Even if a person is caught in some transgression, you who are spiritual should correct that
> one in a gentle spirit, looking to yourself, so that you also may not be tempted. Bear one
> another's burdens, and so you will fulfill the law of Christ.[3]

Rudd seems to say that the African American Catholic community is called to bear the burdens of race. It is called to bear some responsibility for solving some of the problems besetting the African American community. Such words as "leaven" and "bearing burdens" suggest a people not only called upon to make a certain self-sacrifice and self-giving but also possessing a certain vocation. To put it in other words, the Black Catholic community has its own spiritual ethos.

Is There a Black Spirituality?

Spirituality is one of those words that everyone seems to use without precisely defining it. For many Protestants the word means devotion and devotional practices. Catholics, on the other hand, speak of the Inner or Interior Life, the life of the spirit, the life of prayer, or the prayer experience as spirituality. It includes asceticism or discipline, because one cannot pray well without practices that curb the appetites and create good habits or virtues. As we are physical beings, our prayer experience is affected by our language and bodily expression. Whatever may be our ascetical practices, they are always within the context of a given culture. Moreover, whatever may be our cultural environment, the discipline that governs our behavior varies from culture to culture and from people to people. Thus, we speak of classical French spirituality, meaning the writings of Cardinal de Bérulle, St. Francis de Sales, and others of seventeenth-century France. We speak of the school of English spirituality in the fourteenth century, and we think of the *Cloud of Unknowing,* by Richard Rolle, and the *Revelations* of Julian of Norwich. The ways of searching for God and experiencing his presence in our lives is not done within a vacuum but in a cultural context.

For African Americans this context is the African experience lived out in America. Jamie Phelps wrote in an article on African American spirituality:

> Black spirituality is a vital and distinctive spirituality forged in the crucible of the lives of
> various African peoples . . . No matter where or when they live, black people are funda-
> mentally *African* people, whose perspective and way of life have been conditioned by
> their roots in Mother Africa.[4]

---

3. Gal 6:1–2. See also Col 3:13: "Put on then, as God's chosen ones, holy and beloved, heartfelt com-passion, kindness, humility, gentleness, and patience, bearing with one another and forgiving one another."
4. Jamie Phelps, O.P., "Black Spirituality" in *Spiritual Traditions for the Contemporary Church,* ed. Robin Maas and Gabriel O'Donnell, O.P. (Nashville: Abingdon Press, 1990), 332–33.

African Spirituality

Chris Egbulem, a Nigerian Dominican theologian, summarized African spirituality under several basic themes: God is the creator of all and all creation is one and good; life on all levels is God's gift; each person must find one's meaning within the extended family and the community; and within the context of the community the influence of the ancestors and the handing down of the oral tradition also give meaning. To put it another way, African spirituality embraces all creation as good. There is no dualism, no rejection of the physical and the real. God is our father and mother. All things have their origin in God and his presence permeates all things. The individual is incomplete without the extended family and the community. There is a power in the oral tradition; there is a power in the environment in which we live.[5]

This vision of African spirituality with its sense of the holy and the emphasis on God, who is both transcendent and immanent, is a part of that spiritual gift that Pope Paul VI challenged all Africans to give to the whole Catholic Church. Challenging the church of Africa to open itself up to the breadth of the Catholic tradition, he called on Africans to let themselves "be capable of bringing to the Catholic Church the precious and original contribution of 'negritude.'"[6]

The Seven Black Values

African American Catholics sought their connection with what was considered African values in a program known by its Swahili title as the *Nguzo Saba* (Seven Black Values). The original Swahili names are the following:

umoja (unity)
kujichagulia (self-determination)
ujima (collective work and responsibility)
ujamaa (cooperative economics)
nia (purpose)
kuumba (creativity)
imani (faith)

Although these values, with the exception of *imani* (faith), have seemingly very little religious content, some African American Catholics have formulated their own religious meanings. For example, *kujichagulia,* which means self-determination, is connected with the Gospel of Luke 9:51–53, where Jesus turns his face resolutely towards

---

5. Chris Nwaka Egbulem, O.P., "African Spirituality" in *The New Dictionary of Catholic Spirituality* (Collegeville, Minn.: Liturgical Press, 1993).

6. Pope Paul VI, "Top the Heart of Africa," *The Pope Speaks* 14 (1969): 214–20, esp. 219.

Jerusalem. Another Scripture passage connected with self-determination is in Sirach 15:14: "When God in the beginning, created man, he made him subject to his own free choice." This text is especially connected with the vocation awareness aspect of the youth retreats associated with this self-determination.[7]

Many African American Catholic programs do have the merit of making this connection between the *Nguzo Saba* and Scripture. Still, this list of Black values is neither African in origin nor religious in its original meaning. The credit for the *Nguzo Saba* goes to Maulana Karenga,[8] head of the Black Studies Program at California State University at Long Beach, California and director of the African American Cultural Center in Los Angeles. In the 1960s, in the wake of the Black Power movement and the resurgence of Black pride and African culture, Karenga began an intellectual movement known as *Kawaida* (tradition) made up of pan-Africanist thought and socialist ideals. The Black values would serve as the undergirding of this Black nationalist, cultural movement of *Kawaida*.[9] Karenga created *Kwanza*, modeled after an hypothetical African harvest festival. *Kwanza* is celebrated from December 26 to January 1. One Black value is celebrated each day. Special kits are sold with black, green, and red candles and programs. *Kwanza* does not pretend to have any connection with Christmas as a religious celebration.

Is There a Christian Value?

Perhaps it is time for Black Catholics to ask themselves whether Karenga's Seven Black Values are the final word on what Black spirituality should be. Should not there be a more transcendent dimension to Black spirituality? Where is the hunger for God that calls us to enter into the dark cloud of Mount Sinai, where, like Moses, we come face to face with God? Where is that hunger for God that brought Saint Moses the Black to convert from a life of banditry to one of a monk and a priest in the Egyptian desert, becoming one of the first generation of Christian monks and one of the first Black saints.[10]

---

7. See a leaflet, "Celebrating African American History Month Resource Packet" (Louisville: Office of Multicultural Ministry of the Archdiocese of Louisville, 1999). One of the first Catholic efforts to utilize the Seven Black Values for a Black Catholic concept of spirituality is found in A. M. McKnight, C.S.Sp., "A Black Christian Perspective of Spirituality," in *Theology: A Portrait in Black. Proceedings of the Black Catholic Theological Symposium,* no. 1 (Pittsburgh: Capuchin Press, 1980), 103–12. In this article, McKnight indicates that all spirituality must find its roots in Christ but that Black spirituality is "wholistic." This means that it must include the horizontal dimension of concern for one another as Blacks. Our struggle for liberation is not centered in ourselves. In this way the *Nguzo Saba* should serve as a way to live our Christian life in a way that leads to unity and service.

8. Karenga was born Ronald McKinley Everett in 1941. See *Encyclopedia of African-American Culture and History,* s.v. "Karenga, Maulana (Everett, Ronald McKinley)."

9. *Encyclopedia of African-American Culture and History,* s.v. "Kawaida."

10. Saint Moses the Black died around 407 in the Desert of Scete. See Jean-Claude Guy, S.J., *Les Apophtegmes des Péres. Collection Systématique,* chap. I–IX, in *Sources Chrétiennes,* 387 (Paris: Les Éditions du Cerf, 1993), 68–70.

John Mbiti once said that "Africans are notoriously religious."[11] Africans are also notoriously spiritual. This desire for the spiritual was not lost in the Middle Passage; the same characteristic is found among African Americans. It is from this fund of religious spirit that we may find some of the spiritual values that comprise African American Catholic spirituality.

African American Catholic Spirituality: The Virtues

When we talk about values, we are really talking about behavior. Certain kinds of behavior are seen as good. The continual effort to practice more perfectly this good behavior is to acquire a habit of goodness. This habit is what the Scholastic theologians called *virtue*. There are different modes of good behavior, and there are different virtues. The virtues are common to all, but each culture places its own value on each virtue. To live out these virtues in the face of opposition and great hardship is to practice heroic virtue. Those who do so are the saints. That is why a review of the saints of a given people or nation at a particular time in history gives us a picture of a people's spirituality.

What are the virtues that typify the spirituality of a Black people? One such virtue is hospitality, which comes out of a sense of community. One cannot live long in Africa without learning that courtesy and politeness are deeply ingrained in the African cultural systems. That courtesy arises from virtue of hospitality. It is the way Africans learn to relate to others with respect and dignity and contributes to the African respect for the elders. The virtue of hospitality gives rise to magnanimity or generosity, which are clearly important in the African Folktales. Ultimately, hospitality, generosity, and courtesy find their origins in love. The sense of mystery, of God's presence, and of God's power are all the result of reverence—the habit of prayer—which is one of the important aspects of African American spirituality. This sense of prayer, manifested both in the liturgical worship and in private prayer, is evident in Africa both in dance and in the action of full-length prostration before the Blessed Sacrament.

In the same way, African American spirituality is grounded in the experience of prayer. I had the opportunity to participate in a retreat for Black Catholics in the United States. The theme was prayer. Without any prompting or display of reticence, fifty to sixty laypersons began to speak with enthusiasm about the meaning of prayer, about their parents who showed them how to pray, about the place of prayer in their daily lives, about the necessity "to season all things with prayer," about the place of touching others and holding others as we share with others in prayer, and about the importance of surrendering one's whole self to God in prayer.[12] On another occasion, a

---

11. John S. Mbiti, *African Religions and Philosophy* (London: Heinemann, 1969), 1.

12. Cyprian Davis, O.S.B., "Black Spirituality: A Roman Catholic Perspective," *Review and Expositor* 80 (1983): 97–108, esp. 104–106.

ninety-year-old nun from Louisiana described how her Catholic grandmother, a slave, always had her rosary in hand. She prayed the rosary throughout the day and was never found without it. Other nuns in Louisiana explained how their parents, all Catholics, would go into the woods and sing and pray together. In Louisiana, where Black Catholics were segregated within the parish church, a place apart for shared prayer was important.

One salient feature of African American Catholic spirituality is the place of Scripture. Both Black Protestants and Black Catholics utilized Scripture in talks and everyday language. At the Black Catholic Lay Congresses, held from 1889–1894, Black laymen wove allusions to Scripture into their speeches, which Black speakers today would not do. At the 1890 congress held in Cincinnati, William S. Lofton, Black dentist from Washington, D.C., spoke about the need for Catholic education for Black youth. In speaking about racial prejudice in this country, he used the following examples:

> Our efforts would . . . [seem] . . . so fruitless as to provoke only the ridicule of our enemies. But our daily experience, the unquestionable testimony of historians of all ages, and above all the Old and New Testaments, bear witness to the fact that the infinitely perfect God delights to overcome the strong with the weak, the wise with the simple, and if we provoke the sarcastic ridicule of our enemies, let us call to mind the victory of a David over a Goliath.[13]

Addressing the Fourth Black Catholic Congress in 1893, James Spencer of Charleston, South Carolina spoke on the necessity for Black parish churches separate from White parishes, but he concluded with a plea for unity:

> Differing in language, in habit and in taste, we are all united in the bonds of a common religion, having one Lord, one faith, one baptism, one God and Father of all, who is above all and through all and in us all[14]. . . . and [we shall] join in one grand chorus, [in] the beautiful words of Ruth: "Be not against me or desire that I should leave thee and depart, for withersoever thou shalt go I will go, and where thou shalt dwell, I also will dwell; thy people shall be my people, and thy God my God. The land that shall receive thee dying, in the same will I die, and there shall I be buried."[15]

Finally, when Charles Butler addressed the Columbian Catholic Congress in Chicago in 1893 in a talk entitled "The Future of the Negro Race," he too used Scriptural allusions to explain the present situation of the African American. "The history of the [Negroes'] sufferings has been recorded by Him who knows the secrets of all hearts.

---

13. *Three Catholic Afro-American Congresses* (Cincinnati: American Catholic Tribune, 1898; reprint, New York: Arno Press, 1978), 95.

14. Eph 3:5–6.

15. Ru 1:16–17; *St. Joseph's Advocate,* 12th year (1894): 634.

Their sufferings were not unlike the sufferings of the Israelites of old, who were held in bondage for 400 years." He spoke of the mass movement of Blacks to the North as an "exodus" because "[the Negroes] were willing to endure any hardship short of death to reach a land where, under their own vine and fig trees, they could enjoy the life our Creator intended for them."[16]

Saints among Us

One of the contributions made to the American Catholic Church by African American Catholics has been the gift of holiness. Pope John Paul II has beatified and canonized almost a dozen African men and women who lived lives of heroic charity and extraordinary faith. Saint Martin de Porres, canonized by Pope John XXIII in 1962, lived and worked in Lima, Peru, where he died in 1639. He was a man who displayed immense charity in a life of service and in his profession of healing given freely to all who asked. He was a servant in the Dominican Convent there. Dispensing alms, healing, and aid, he reached out to all with humor, concern, and love. Two centuries later in New York City, a former slave from Haiti, the Venerable Pierre Toussaint, who died in 1853, left the memory of unceasing charity shown to others—to homeless Black orphans, to the aristocratic women whose hair he dressed, to the many people to whom he gave a home, a refuge, and money. He did it with humor and grace. All revered him as a saint.

Likewise, two Black American women have had their causes for sainthood introduced in Rome. One, Elizabeth Lange, founded the Oblate Sisters of Providence in 1829 in order to begin a school in Baltimore for the education of girls and later for boys. She founded a community that became the home for the Baltimore Black Catholic community. Service to others was the keynote of the life of Henriette Delille, a free woman of color in New Orleans, who began her community of pious women in the 1840s to serve aged ex-slaves thrown on the mercies of a society that had no place for them. Henriette's community cared for them and many others who found an asylum known as the hospice of the Holy Family, which eventually became the name of the growing community of religious women—the Sisters of the Holy Family. Their service was to the poor, their teaching for young girls of color, and their courses in catechetics for the slaves.

Conclusion

Is this Black Catholic spirituality, homegrown on American soil, significantly different from the spirituality of White American Catholics? Probably not, but looked at in another way, the answer is a resounding "yes." Daniel Rudd thought that Black

---

16. *The World's Columbian Catholic Congresses* (Chicago: J. S. Hyland and Company, 1893), 123.

Catholics had a call to be a "leaven" among Black Americans. As Catholics in what many thought to be a White church, they had a particular burden to bear. As Catholics, they were often neglected; as enslaved, they helped build a church; as parishioners they were forced to the back of the same churches. Still, as Catholics they sang their own songs, prayed in their own cadenced phrases, and practiced their own virtues. They found their own space in a sometimes hostile brand of Catholicism, into which their own spirit was bathed with God's grace and thereby enriched the spirituality of the Catholic Church in America today.

We've Come This Far by Faith: Black Catholics and Their Church

Diana L. Hayes

The Black Catholic bishops of the United States issued their first and, to date, only pastoral letter, "What We Have Seen and Heard," [1] in 1984. They did so in recognition of their belief that "the Black Catholic community in the American Church has now come of age." This coming of age, they noted, "brings with it the duty, the privilege and the joy to share with others the rich experience of the 'Word of Life.'"[2]

Today, we are witnesses to further signs of that coming of age. We African American Catholics[3] are claiming our rightful place in the Roman Catholic Church, nationally and globally. Basing our claim for recognition and inclusion on our history in the American church that predates the Mayflower, our persistent faith gives living expression to the "Word of Life" that we have received and that we fully embrace:

> You are no longer strangers and sojourners, but you are fellow citizens with the saints and members of the household of God, built upon the foundation of the apostles and prophets, Christ Jesus himself being the cornerstone, in whom the whole structure is joined together and grows into a holy temple in the Lord; in whom you also are built into it for a dwelling place of God in the Spirit (Eph 2:19–22).

Strangers and sojourners no longer, African American Catholics will no longer be required, in the words of the Psalmist, to "sing the Lord's song in a foreign land" (Ps 137, *NRSV*). Instead, we are taking down our harps and converting that "foreign land" into a homeland, one rich with the woven tapestries of our voices, lifted in praise and song;

This article is taken from Diana L. Hayes and Cyprian Davis, O.S. B., eds., *Taking Down Our Harps: Black Catholics in the United States* (Maryknoll, N.Y.: Orbis, 1998). Republished with permission.

1. Cincinnati, Ohio: St. Anthony Messenger Press, 1984.

2. Ibid., 2.

3. In this work, the terms "African American Catholic" and "Black Catholic" will be used interchangeably to depict Catholics of African descent now living in the United States, whether their arrival in this country lies in the distant past or in the present.

of our spirituality expressed in deep and heartfelt prayer and preaching; and of our cultural heritage—a colorful mixture of peoples of Africa, the Caribbean, the West Indies, South America, and North America.

Evidence of this new-found land can be seen throughout the United States today in dioceses large and small, rural, urban and suburban; all blessed and invigorated by the presence and spirit of Black Catholics who are busy about the work of Jesus Christ. We are seeking, in Jesus' name, to "preach good news to the poor, . . . to proclaim release to the captives, and recovering of sight to the blind, to set at liberty those who are oppressed, to proclaim the acceptable year of the Lord" (Lk 4:18–19). For in their holistic world view all of life is necessarily interconnected; the sacred and the secular, the workplace and the Church, are all umbued with the spirit of God and thus are the responsibility of people of faith.

A New Birth

In many ways the voices of these new and yet-so-old Catholics can be understood as calling forth a new witness. We see ourselves as "a chosen race, a royal priesthood, a holy nation, God's own people" who work to "declare the wonderful deeds of him who called [us] out of darkness into his marvelous light." Throughout our existence in the United States we were seen as "no people," but today African American Catholics affirm that we "are God's people"; once little mercy was given us "but now [we] have received mercy" from God on high (1 Pt 2:9–10).

As part of that witness we recognize the necessity of exposing the inaccurate education received by all, of whatever race, who dwell in this land regarding the contributions of our Black and Catholic foremothers and forefathers to the present status of the United States. The truth of our history, both in this and other adopted lands and in our motherland as well, must be recovered, for that history reveals the proud and distinctive heritage that is ours, one which predates the Greek and Roman empires as well as Christopher Columbus. We Black Catholics must also tell our story within our Church, a story which has as part of its richness a cherished role in the life of the Church dating back to Africa. For it was our African foremothers and forefathers who received the teachings of Christ from the Church's earliest beginnings; they who nurtured and sheltered those teachings, preserving them from the depredations of those still pagan; they who received, revitalized, and rechristianized those teachings, too often distorted at the hands of their would-be masters, in the new lands of the Americas. As Father Cyprian Davis has written of those early years of African history:

> Long before Christianity arrived in the Scandinavian countries, at least a century before
> St. Patrick evangelized Ireland, and over two centuries before St. Augustine would arrive
> in Canterbury, and almost seven centuries before the conversion of the Poles and the es-
> tablishment of the kingdom of Poland, this mountainous Black kingdom [Ethiopia] was a

Catholic nation with its own liturgy, its own spectacular religious art, its own monastic tradition, its saints, and its own spirituality.[4]

This cherished heritage must, once again, be brought forth, exposed to the light of a new day, and shared with all of the Catholic Church.

Arguably, one can say that the continued presence of Black Catholics in the Catholic Church in the United States serves as a subversive memory, one which turns all of reality upside-down, for it is a memory of hope brought forth from pain, of perseverance maintained in the face of bloody opposition, and of faith born of tortured struggle. It is the memory of a people forced to bring forth life from conditions conducive only to death, much as Christ himself was restored to life after a scandalous death. Ours is a memory of survival against all odds. It is the memory of a people, born in a strange and often hostile land, paradoxically celebrating Christ's victory over death as a sign of God's promise of their eventual liberation from a harsh servitude imposed by their fellow Christians. Today, we Black Catholics are affirming that we are no longer sojourners, we are no longer just passing through; we are here to stay and intend to celebrate our presence as only we can.

The Persistent Presence of Racism

This memory becomes even more challenging when we recognize the demographic shifts taking place both in the United States and in the Roman Catholic Church as we enter upon the third millennium. The most recent U.S. Census statistics present a picture of a very different American society and American Catholic Church, one in which persons of color, as a whole, are the majority rather than the minority. African American Catholics will be a part of this majority, which can be seen, depending on one's perspective, as threatening to the very stability and identity of both church and state or simply as a sign of the changing times that must be dealt with.

These changes do provide a critical challenge for us as Church today as we seek to affirm the new understandings of theology, ministry, and liturgy that are already emerging from persons heretofore marginalized on the Church's periphery. Black Catholic theology is only one example of these shifts in understanding that must be acknowledged and placed in dialogue within the academy and the Church. This theology was born out of the struggle to maintain both our Catholic faith and our Black culture in the face of the racism that still besets our Church, institutionally and individually. The Pontifical Peace and Justice Commission noted in 1989:

---

4. Cyprian Davis, O.S.B., "Black Spirituality: A Catholic Perspective," in *One Faith, One Lord, One Baptism: The Hopes and Experiences of the Black Community in the Archdiocese of New York*, vol. 2 (New York: Archdiocese of New York: Office of Pastoral Research, 1988), 45.

Today racism has not disappeared. There are even troubling new manifestations of it here and there in various forms, be they spontaneous, officially tolerated or institutionalized. . . . The victims are certain groups of persons whose physical appearance or ethnic, cultural or religious characteristics are different from those of the dominant group and are interpreted by the latter as being signs of innate and definite inferiority, thereby justifying all discriminatory practices in their regard.[5]

Racism is a fact of life that continues to torment Black Americans regardless of their particular faith. It has its roots in the very foundations of our society, where, in drafting the Constitution, the enslavement of Blacks was recognized and accepted. The revolutionary phrases of the Founding Fathers, proclaiming liberty and justice for all and declaring the equality of all "men," ignored the condition of Black humanity. As the late Supreme Court Justice Thurgood Marshall noted, "The famous first three words of that document, 'We the People,' did not include women who were denied the vote, or blacks, who were enslaved."[6] The intent was clearly expressed in the notification that Blacks counted as only three-fifths of a White person and then only for the purpose of White male representation in the new Congress. The Constitution was developed not as a color-blind document but as one assuring the hegemony of White, propertied males over all others living in the newly formed union.

Racism has changed its face, however. Rather than the blatant overt racism of prior years, today we are confronted with a more sinister, because less visible, form of covert racism. Institutional racism "originates in the operation of established and respected forces in the society and thus receives far less public consideration."[7]

As such, institutional racism is more than a form "sanctioned by the Constitution and laws of a country,"[8] as the Vatican commission suggests. For even after that Constitution has been expunged of its color bias, and the laws mandating segregation and second-class citizenship have been removed, the aura of institutionalized racism still persists. It persists in the very warp and woof of that society which has, for so long, been imbued with an ideology supported all too often by an erroneous interpretation of the teachings of Sacred Scripture.

The 1960s and 1970s saw significant changes in the laws governing American society with regard to African Americans. Yet, today, many of those changes are being nullified and labeled as preferential treatment, thereby ignoring the centuries of slavery and second-class citizenship that have hindered the descendants of African slaves from attaining equal opportunity before the law. All too often persons of faith have been silent in the face of these assaults against the human dignity of persons of color.

---

5. "The Church and Racism: Toward a More Fraternal Society," *Origins* 18:37 (February 23, 1989): 617.

6. In Janet Dewart, ed., *The State of Black America 1988* (New York: National Urban League, 1988), 6.

7. S. Carmichael and C. V. Hamilton, *Black Power: The Politics of Liberation in America* (New York: Vintage Books, 1967), 4.

8. "The Church and Racism," 617.

Racism still persists. It is a mindset that flies in the face of Sacred Scripture and the teachings of the Christian church. It is a distortion of the teaching that "all are endowed with a rational soul and are created in God's image."[9] Racism is incompatible with God's design. It is a sin that goes beyond the individual acts of individual human beings. Racism, to be blunt, is sin that becomes a constituent part of the framework of society, sin that is the concentration to the infinite of the personal sins of those who condone evil.

The U.S. Catholic bishops have affirmed this understanding:

> The structures of our society are subtly racist, for these structures reflect the values which society upholds. They are geared to the success of the majority and the failure of the minority. Members of both groups give unwitting approval by accepting things as they are. Perhaps no single individual is to blame. The sinfulness is often anonymous but nonetheless real. The sin is social in nature in that each of us in some measure are accomplices. . . . The absence of personal fault for an evil does not absolve one of all responsibility. We must seek to resist and undo injustices we have not caused, lest we become bystanders who tacitly endorse evil and so share in guilt for it.[10]

Reflecting on the Journey

Theology, in its simplest understanding, can be seen as "God-talk." We, as African American Catholics, often become intimidated when asked to reflect theologically on a matter of importance to us, such as our relationship with God or how we see our role in the Church, because we see ourselves as academically unqualified. There are too few of us with academic degrees in systematic theology.[11] Yet, when asked to simply talk about God's action in our lives or the working of the Holy Spirit in our midst, our reaction is quite different.

Although the world of academe may not recognize our reflections as such, we are indeed speaking theologically when we do this. And as African Americans, we have been doing so for all of our existence. What we have done, as a holistic people in whom the sacred and secular are intertwined rather than alienated, is simply to talk about God, about Jesus Christ, about the Holy Spirit and about their importance in our lives, a God that you can lean on, a brother you can depend on in your darkest hours, a Spirit who walks with you and brings peace to a troubled soul. We have not put our theology down in dry, dusty tomes that no one can or really wants to read; we have lived it in the midst

---

9. Vatican II, *Gaudium et Spes*, no. 29.

10. National Conference of Catholic Bishops, *Brothers and Sisters to Us: The U.S. Bishops' Pastoral Letter on Racism in Our Day* (Washington, D.C.: United States Catholic Conference, 1979), 3.

11. At this time, there are six Black Catholic theologians with terminal degrees in systematic theology. They are the Most Reverend Edward Braxton, S.T.D.; M. Shawn Copeland, Ph.D.; Diana L. Hayes, S.T.D.; Philip Linden, S.S.J., S.T.D.; Jamie Phelps, O.P., Ph.D.; and Reverend Bryan N. Massingale, S.T.D. The number of Black Catholics with degrees in other theological/religious studies areas is growing, however.

of our daily lives. That theology has been expressed most clearly in our songs, in our stories, in our prayers. We talk of a God who saves, a God who preserves, a God who frees and continues to free us from the "troubles of this world."

Theology also can be seen as "interested conversation." In other words, theology is talk, dialogue, discussion, conversation about God and God's salvific action in the world, not from an objective, unbiased stance—because no such stance truly exists—but from the perspective of one who is "involved," one who is caught up in that discussion, one whose involvement is "colored," as it were, by his or her own history, heritage, and culture. We cannot speak about the Church, Jesus Christ or anything else except from within the context of who we are, a people caught in a daily struggle to survive despite the constant assaults of racism, prejudice, and discrimination from the institutional structures of both our society and our Church.

This is to say, on one hand, that there are as many different theologies within the Church as there are persons talking about God, but, on the other hand, that all of these theologies have, as their foundation, the context of Roman Catholicism with its particular teachings, traditions, and faith beliefs. Our theology as African American Catholics is "interested conversation" about that "ultimate reality" which is central to the core of our being, our faith in Jesus Christ. As such, it cannot be understood or conceived of apart from our being and the place in which we find ourselves. All theologies are particular, rooted in and arising from a particular context, the context of the people engaged in their development. Theology arises out of their loves and their angers, their joys and their sorrows, their sufferings and their hopes for a better tomorrow as they express these in the light of their faith.

Today, we, as an African American Catholic people, are engaged in the development of a theology that speaks truly to us and expresses who we are and whose we are for the enlightenment of the entire Church.

We are African Americans: a people with roots deeply sunk in the history and culture of our African homeland yet also a people with a long and proud history in these United States. Both strands of our heritage are important in defining who we are. Neither can be denied without denying an important part of our very selves. That understanding of "who we are and whose we are" affects our theologizing. It "colors," quite simply, our concept of God, our faith in Jesus Christ, our existence in the Holy Spirit, our total understanding of what it means to be truly Black and authentically Catholic. Our reflections are not abstract or objective; they are particular because they are grounded in the particular context of African American history, which is a history of slavery, of second-class citizenship, of discrimination, both in U.S. society and our mother Church as well. More importantly, it is also a history of struggle, of perseverance, of hope, of faith, and of survival against all odds and all obstacles placed in our path.

As a holistic people, however, the pain does not outweigh the hope, the struggle does not diminish the faith. We rejoice in the intertwining, rather than the separation, of the many strands of our life, for we are a people for whom religious faith has been and remains an integral part of who and what we are. Thus, the context of our theologizing is a grounding in our faith, examined in the light of Christ's teachings and a religious tradition dating back to the early Church. Accordingly, our lives must be a witness to the ongoing and pervasive presence of the gospel within us and must reflect that presence back into the world in which we live.

We therefore cherish our memories, painful though they may often be, for they serve as subversive memories, memories that turn all of reality upside-down, as Jesus Christ did in his life, death, and resurrection. These memories transform that which is seen as worthless to that which is of the highest value. We remember, not with an eye toward revenge but in order to prevent faintheartedness in the struggle. We remember that we, as a people, survived and continue to survive despite it all. The apostle Paul's words have a particular significance for us: "God chose what is foolish in the world to shame the wise, God chose what is weak in the world to shame the strong, God chose what is low and despised in the world, even things that are not, to bring to nothing things that are" (1Cor 1:27–28).

We have been, and too often continue to be, seen as the "low and despised" in the world in which we find ourselves, but paradoxically we see ourselves also as that chosen race and priestly people commissioned to overturn the inaccurate education of ourselves and all Americans regarding African Americans. Knowledge and understanding of our chosenness comes to us from our God, who nurtured and sustained us like a bridge over the troubled waters of our sojourn here. It is from God that we received our faith, and it is to God that we turn in the bosom of our Church, the Roman Catholic Church. For it is the Church that our foremothers and forefathers nurtured and sustained long before many who now claim total ownership of it even knew of its existence.

Black Catholics have remained in the Church, feeling both love and hate, forgiveness and frustration, concern and impatience. We, too, the darker brothers and sisters of this country, are a vital and vibrant part of the Roman Catholic Church. We, too, have gifts of song, story, and praise to offer the Church universal. And we know that those gifts are not only needed but welcomed by the number of our Catholic brothers and sisters who attend our services of worship and even join our gospel choirs, recognizing, perhaps, the absence in their lives of a joy-filled praise of God that brings a comforting peace.

Yet, still, we wonder at the coldness with which we are so often received, and at the anger that is directed toward us. How do we prove that we are who we say we are? Why must we even do so? As W. E. B. Du Bois recognized almost a century ago, African Americans, and especially African American Catholics are often caught in a quandary. He states:

> It is a peculiar sensation, this double consciousness, this sense of always looking at one's self through the eyes of others, of measuring one's soul by the tape of a world that looks on in amused contempt and pity. One ever feels his twoness—an American, a Negro; two

souls, two thoughts, two unreconciled strivings; two warring ideals in one dark body, whose dogged strength alone keeps it from being torn asunder.[12]

This has been our quandary in the four hundred years of our sojourn in this land. But the confusion is now at end; the turmoil is over; the strivings are reconciled. There is evidence throughout this nation that our Catholic African American sisters and brothers are taking down their harps from the walls, they are taking them out of the dark trunks and closets where they have been gathering the dust of the ages and are proclaiming, as our poetic brother did years ago, that we, too, sing America.

We are proclaiming to the Church and the world at large that to be Black and Catholic is not a paradox; it is not a conflict; it is not a contradiction. To be Black and Catholic is correct, it is authentic, it is who we are and have always been. For, ironically, it must also be recognized that questions about our faithfulness have come not just from our Catholic family but from the greater Black community. This is further evidence of the critical need for the full history of the African presence in early Christianity as well as in the United States predating the English-speaking Protestant colonies to be told. For in so telling, naysayers will have to acknowledge that there have been African peoples in the Catholic Church as long as that Church has existed. Black faith is not and cannot be limited to one church or one expression. But it does share in a richness of heritage that predates Christianity and continues to shape and form it into a new creation.

The time finally has come for African American Catholics to articulate fully our self-understanding and to present that articulation not only to our brothers and sisters in the Roman Catholic Church but to all with whom we come into contact. If theology is "God-talk," if it is "interested conversation," then we must become full and active participants in that conversation, one which has been going on for too long a time without our input.

In our gatherings, discussions, dialogues, days of reflection, revivals, and congresses we are developing a theology, a way of speaking about God, Jesus, the Holy Spirit, the Church and all that pertains to them in a way that is indigenous to us, that is Afri-centric, that is truly Black and authentically Catholic. Our way of doing theology stems from our understanding of and faith in a God who is an active, interested, and loving participant in our history.

We say this not to be divisive, not to deny the truths and teachings of our Catholic faith, but simply to acknowledge for ourselves and to demand from others the recognition of our distinctive Catholicity, a Catholicity with African roots and myriad branches.

---

12. W. E. B. Du Bois, "Of Our Spiritual Strivings," in *The Souls of Black Folk* (New York: NAL [Signet Classics], 1969), 45.

Speaking the Truth

It is time to "speak the truth to the people."[13] It is time for the history of the darker peoples of the Catholic Church to be set forth so that all can learn not only of the dark days of colonization and enslavement but also of the days of civilizations ancient and renowned throughout the world. Instead of others' stories, we must learn of and share our stories so that we see ourselves as a new people empowered by our knowledge to take our rightful place in the ranks of peoples of the world. Pope Paul VI noted when in Africa that we, as Africans and people of African descent, are now missionaries to ourselves. He stated further: "You must now give your gifts of Blackness to the whole church,"[14] a sentiment reaffirmed by Pope John Paul II in his meeting with Black Catholics in 1987.

We must learn of ourselves and then share that knowledge with others. "We have come this far by faith," in the words of our gospel heritage, and we will and must continue to explore and uncover the truth of our past so that we may move forward into the future.

African American Catholics have retained, despite the strains of slavery, segregation, discrimination, and second-class citizenship, a steadfast faith in God. Remaining unseduced by the distortions of Christianity force-fed them during slavery, they have always believed in a God who saves, one who was on the side of the poor and oppressed, like them. This steadfast faith in a God who promised eventual deliverance grounds all that is said and done, providing thereby a freedom, both spiritual and physical, for there is no dichotomy between the life lived on earth and the life to be lived with the coming of the Kingdom.

In order to learn of ourselves, in order to understand and accept "who and whose" we are, we must reflect on both faith and its praxis, seeking to understand for ourselves, in language of our own choosing, the constant presence of God within our lives while recognizing with St. Anselm that theology in its truest sense is "faith seeking understanding." We must then share that understanding with all of the Church. For it is in learning the "truth" of ourselves that we are empowered to continue the struggle, "leaning on the everlasting arms" of our God.

Plenty Good Room

We are all called to defend the faith that is ours (I Pt 3:15). This is especially true on the local level, for it is in the parish setting that we are called upon to spread the gospel

---

13. Mari Evans, "Speak the Truth to the People," in *Trouble the Water: 250 Years of African-American Poetry,* ed. Jerry W. Ward, Jr. (New York and London: Mentor, Penguin Group, 1997), 217–219.

14. "To the Heart of Africa" (address to the bishops of the African Continent at the closing session of a symposium held in Kampala, Uganda), in *The Pope Speaks* 14 (1969), 219.

of Jesus Christ, both in and outside of the Church itself. We are all called as Christian faithful who have been anointed in baptism to share in the mission and ministry of Christ (canon 204). It is our responsibility and our joy to evangelize, to spread the good news of the life, death, and resurrection of our Lord and Savior Jesus Christ to all around us. This must be done for those outside the Church but even more so for those within. We must rekindle the spirit of love within the hearts of our brothers and sisters in Christ. But we must do so in a way that is uniquely ours. As a people of God, we are called to witness to the working of the Holy Spirit within us, while recognizing the different gifts which the Spirit has bestowed.

It is the Spirit of God which has empowered us as African American Catholics to speak of our faith and to present that faith without shame, recognizing that as African American Catholics, we are "no longer simply recipients of the ministry of others, [but] are called to be full participants in the life and mission of the Church, on both the local and national levels."[15]

It is now time for African American Catholics to take ownership of this Church in which they have for so long lived marginalized and often alienated lives. We are called to express that ownership in all that we say and do, in our workshops, programs, liturgies, parishes, and every part of our lives.

Today we recognize and affirm that to be both Black and Catholic is not a contradiction but a proclamation of historical pride, for to be truly Black and authentically Catholic means that we, as an African and American and Catholic people, have, indeed, come of age and are beginning to act in accordance with our adulthood. It means that we are challenging the all-too-prevalent understanding of Roman Catholicism as a Western, Euro-centric religion. We are proclaiming by our presence in the Church that there is, indeed, "plenty good room" in our Father's Kingdom for a diversity of expressions of the Catholic faith. We are challenging the Church Catholic to acknowledge that recognition and acceptance of the cultures and heritages of the many peoples who make up the Church, as they are lived out in the faith and worship of these people, are no longer luxuries but a necessities. Otherwise, there is the risk of preaching not the transcendent Christ, but a cultural Christ, one who is embodied in a particular time, a particular context, a particular culture.

As the Church finally opens itself to the contributions of peoples of every race and ethnicity, it must also expand its understanding and expression of God and Jesus Christ. This correlates with our understanding of the incarnation of Jesus Christ. If God became incarnate in a human being, a male, a Jew, taking on all of the characteristics and appearances of that humanity, so must the Church, expressive of Christ's body, incarnate itself today in the peoples and cultures with whom it has come in contact. This is not optional; it is mandated.

---

15. "Here I Am, Send Me: The U.S. Bishops' Response to the Evangelization of African Americans and the National Black Catholic Pastoral Plan," *Origins* 19:30 (December 28, 1989), 487.

There is "plenty good room" in God's Kingdom. We must only choose our seats and sit down. As African American Catholics, however, we must ensure not only that we are doing the choosing but that the seats actually "fit" us, that we have participated fully in their construction and placement at the center, not the periphery, of our Church.

As Black Catholics we are full members of the Catholic communion. We have struggled for a long time, but the journey is nearing its end. As we continue towards that end, we take as our mandate the words of the prophet Isaiah: "They who wait upon the Lord shall renew their strength, they shall mount up with wings like eagles, they shall run and not be weary, they shall walk and not faint" (40:31). Our faith has not faltered, and our Spirit has been renewed. We are truly Black and authentically Catholic. As we continue to deepen our own understanding of ourselves, we offer the gift of ourselves to the Roman Catholic Church, acknowledging that there is still much work to be done. Yet, we have come this far by faith, and that faith will in time lead us home.

The Emergence of African American Catholic Worship

Mary E. McGann and Eva Marie Lumas

T he religious and social ferment created in the 1960s by Vatican II and the African American Civil Rights movement set the stage for momentous change for Black Catholics in the United States. In the years following these events, the American Church has witnessed the emergence of distinctively African American patterns of celebrating Catholic worship. This article will trace the process by which these new expressions of Catholic liturgy have been forged over the past four decades. It will identify the historical forces that served as catalysts; the leadership that has guided the process; the issues, both liturgical and contextual, that have given it direction; the cultural self-redefinition among African American Catholics that has shaped and fostered the reclaiming of a distinct "ethno-religious patrimony" within the larger Church; and the present and future challenges to this process.

Historian Cyprian Davis has brilliantly traced the long history of African American Catholics in the United States.[1] The earliest baptismal records from St. Augustine, Florida, dating from the second half of the sixteenth century, attest to the presence of Catholics of African descent. Likewise, their presence is evident in Spanish, French, and English-speaking territories during the American colonial period.[2] The history of Black Catholics in the United States is one of loyalty and contribution, of frustration and marginalization. As early as 1889, African American lay Catholics gave birth to an indigenous tradition of struggle for social justice.[3] Through a series of National Black Catholic Lay Congresses, held between 1889 and 1894, Catholics of African descent worked "to enjoy the [full] heritage of their faith; to win for themselves, their progeny,

---

1. Cyprian Davis, *The History of Black Catholics in the United States* (New York: Crossroad, 1990).

2. Cyprian Davis, "Evangelization and Culture in the Historical Context of Black America," in *Our Roots and Gifts* (Washington, D.C.: Archdiocese of Washington, 1989), 109–114. See also Davis, *History of Black Catholics*.

3. M. Shawn Copeland, "African American Catholics and Black Theology: An Interpretation," in *Black Theology, A Documentary History, Vol. II: 1980–1992,* ed. James H. Cone and Gayraud S. Wilmore (Maryknoll, N.Y.: Orbis, 1993), 99–115.

and their people, the attention, care and respect of the Church; and to help secure the rights of citizenship for their race."[4] Yet, despite their committed engagement in the life of the Church, Black Catholics were systematically excluded from clerical leadership.

Black involvement in Catholic liturgical life was likewise marked by loyalty and frustration. While valuing the sacramental character of Catholic worship, many Black members suffered from liturgies that were dry, uninspired, staid, and lacking in the deep religious feeling that could nourish and express their spiritual longings. In the words of Glen Jeanmarie, "when our people embraced the Catholic faith, they rejected their past in order to become a 'new creation'. . . . [They] left behind Blackness and became pure, White, and Catholic."[5] Cyprian Rowe points out that

> Catholics of African descent have suffered intensely from the sterility of liturgical rites because they have somewhere in their bones a tradition of worship in which the sung and spoken word have been fused into celebrations of joy. Afro-Americans are therefore among the first to realize that it is a certain cultural ignorance, and even cultural imperialism, that have resulted in their almost total exclusion from worship, except as spectators.[6]

As faithful and loyal participants in the Catholic tradition, Black Catholics shared another cultural-religious legacy, a tradition well described as "African-American Christianity."[7] This indigenous form of Christian life exceeded the boundaries of any church body, penetrating the fabric of life within the Black community in the United States.[8] African American Christianity was born of the Black struggle for liberation, freedom, and wholeness in situations of oppression. In pursuing liberation, Black Americans had found "a great Savior, Jesus Christ, the Emancipator."[9] Within the crucible of non-Catholic Christian churches, they forged a distinctive style of Christian worship rooted in the expressive patterns of African ritual and expressed through music, preaching, prayer, and testimony.[10] Black Catholics, while participating in Catholic parish life, shared and were nourished by this larger Black religious heritage.

---

4. Ibid., 99. The First Black Catholic Lay Congress was held in Washington, D.C. in 1889. Other congresses were 1890, Cincinnati; 1892, Philadelphia; 1893, Chicago; and 1894, Baltimore.

5. Glenn V. Jeanmarie, "Black Catholic Worship: Celebrating Roots and Wings," in *Theology: A Portrait in Black,* ed. Thaddeus Posey, O.F.M. Cap. (Pittsburgh: Capuchin Press, 1980), 80.

6. Cyprian L. Rowe, "The Case for a Distinctive Black Culture," in *This Far by Faith: American Black Worship and Its African Roots,* ed. National Office for Black Catholics (Washington, D.C.: Liturgical Conference, 1977), 27.

7. See D. R. Whitt, "*Varietates Legitimae* and an African-American Liturgical Tradition," *Worship* 71, no. 6 (1997): 504–537.

8. See Melva Wilson Costen, *African American Christian Worship* (Nashville:Abingdon Press, 1993).

9. William B. McClain, "The Black Religious Experience in the United States," in *This Far By Faith: American Black Worship and Its African Roots,* ed. National Office for Black Catholics (Washington, D.C.: Liturgical Conference, 1977), 37.

10. Wilton D. Gregory, "Black Catholic Liturgy: What Do You Say It Is?," *U.S. Catholic Historian* 7, nos. 2 and 3 (1988): 317.

Yet this "patrimony" was systematically excluded from their expression of Catholic worship.[11]

The 1960s: A Kairos Moment for Black Catholics

The convergence of the African American Civil Rights movement and Vatican II in the 1960s set Black Catholics and the entire American Church on a new course. Theologian M. Shawn Copeland identifies the intersection of these two events as a *kairos*[12] moment for African American Catholics.

> Change in the social mood without change in the ecclesial mood might have forced Black Catholics in the United States to abandon their centuries-old religious tradition; change in the ecclesial mood without change in the social mood might have compelled them to barter their racial-cultural heritage for silver. There was a propitiousness to these times. This was God's time: this was *kairos*.[13]

On the one hand, the Civil Rights movement challenged the structures of social and economic segregation of Blacks in the United States. It gave birth to a new cultural consciousness, a pride in their God-given worth, that challenged the negative Black identity that had been reinforced in American culture and in the Church itself.[14] It awakened in Black Catholics a renewed sense of their religious and ritual heritage that had yet to find expression in Catholic life and worship and called into question the persistent racism that denied them full participation and leadership in the Church. In the late 1960s, the first National Black Catholic Clergy Caucus (NBCCC) gathered to address the American bishops on urgent issues that faced the Black community.[15] This initial act of national solidarity among Black clergy was quickly followed by other initiatives to foster Black leadership—clerical, religious, episcopal, and lay.[16] In turn, the new leadership that emerged in the 1960s became highly significant in the unfolding of African American Catholic liturgy.

---

11. See Ronald L. Sharpes, "Black Catholic Gifts of Faith," *U.S. Catholic Historian* 15, no. 4 (1997): 35–41. For the significance of the term "patrimony," see Whitt, *"Varietates Legitimae."*

12. *Kairos* as used by Paul in the New Testament refers to a "ecisive moment," "a time rich in opportunity," or "eschatologically filled time." See Horst Balz and Gerhard Schneider, eds., *Exegetical Dictionary of the New Testament* (Grand Rapids: William B. Eerdmans, 1981), 232–233.

13. Copeland, "African American Catholics," 101.

14. Edward K. Braxton, "We, Too, Sing America," in *Our Roots and Gifts* (Washington, D.C.: Archdiocese of Washington, 1989), 91. See also Sharpes, "Black Catholic Gifts," 37.

15. In response to their demands, the U.S. Catholic bishops issued a "Statement on Race" (1968), but neither this document, nor its predecessor, "Discrimination and the Christian Conscience" (1958), fully redressed the persistent inequality experienced by African American Catholics.

16. The formation of the NBCCC was followed almost immediately by the organization of the National Black Sisters' Conference.

Within the same decade, the Second Vatican Council challenged the historic cultural, intellectual, and theological insularity of the Catholic Church. The council modeled in an historic way a church that desires to embrace all cultures and articulated a vision of a worldwide church that "respects and fosters the genius and talents of various races and peoples."[17] In embracing a new ecclesial vision, one in which no single culture can be normative for Catholic life and worship, council leaders set a far-reaching course for liturgical inculturation:

> Even in the liturgy the Church has no wish to impose a rigid uniformity. . . rather, the Church respects and fosters the genius and talents of various races and peoples. The Church . . . preserves intact the elements of these people's way of life . . . and admits such elements into the liturgy itself, provided they are in keeping with the true and authentic spirit of the liturgy. . . . Provisions shall be made . . . for legitimate variations and adaptations to different groups, regions, and peoples. . . . In some places and circumstances . . . an even more radical adaptation of the liturgy is needed.[18]

Following the council, two pontiffs gave explicit invitations to Catholics in Africa and of African descent to share their religious-cultural heritage with the Church. Pope Paul VI, in his 1969 address in Kampala, invited the churches of Africa to bring "to the Catholic Church the precious and original contribution of 'Blackness' which she particularly needs in this historic hour."[19] His call was taken to refer to Blacks throughout the African diaspora and was often quoted to assert the cause of the Black Catholic movement in the United States. Several years later, John Paul II addressed representatives of the African American Catholic community in New Orleans: "your Black cultural heritage enriches the Church and makes her witness of universality more complete."[20]

Reverend Clarence R. Joseph Rivers and the Beginnings of a "Black Renaissance" in Catholic Church Liturgy

Coinciding with the council's welcome of diverse cultural expression, Rev. Clarence R. Joseph Rivers was launching what would become a "Black Renaissance" in

---

17. Vatican Council II, *Pastoral Constitution on the Church in the Modern World* (Washington, D.C.: USCC Publishing Office, 1965), nos. 53–62; Vatican Council II, *Constitution on the Sacred Liturgy*, in *The Liturgy Documents,* 3rd ed. (Chicago: Liturgy Training Publications, 1991), no. 37.

18. *Constitution on the Sacred Liturgy*, nos. 37–38, 40. Subsequent conciliar and postconciliar documents restate and develop these principles.

19. Address given in Kampala, 31 July 1969. Quoted in Black Catholic Bishops of the United States, *What We Have Seen and Heard: A Pastoral Letter on Evangelization from the Black Bishops of the United States* (Cincinnati: St. Anthony Messenger, 1984), 3.

20. Pope John Paul II, "The Pope's Address to Black Catholics," New Orleans, La., 12 Sept. 1987. See also *Origins* 24 Sept. 1987, 252.

American Catholic liturgy.[21] Rivers, a musician, dramatist, author, scholar, liturgist, and composer, was convinced that the treasury of African American art, culture, and religious expression could revitalize Catholic worship. Several years before Vatican II, Rivers began composing liturgical music in a Black idiom, producing his *American Mass Program* in 1963.[22] In his compositions, Rivers drew on the spirituals, jazz, and gospel, thus introducing American Catholics to the rhythms, melodies, and harmonies of the Black musical idiom. Other composers, notably Eddie Bonnemere and Mary Lou Williams, joined Rivers in the attempt to bring the full range of Black music to Catholic worship. However, their use of jazz, calypso, and gospel in liturgical music was not always accepted and at times openly resisted.[23]

Through workshops and lectures, Rivers worked "to bring greater cultural coherence to the liturgy" by "critically reexamine[ing] the relation of the various elements of the Mass to the Black idiom."[24] In so doing, he began to articulate a specifically African American Catholic liturgical aesthetic, an aesthetic that required (1) the use of drums, highly rhythmic music, musical improvisation, and dance; (2) a ritualized but spontaneous participation of the worshiping community, free of rubrical rigidity; and (3) rich poetic preaching and prayer that draw on participatory drama. This aesthetic is rooted in a theology that knows God to be both transcendent and immanent and flows from a spirituality in which "to be spiritual is to be alive, to be capable of moving and of responding to movement."[25] In 1968, Rivers founded Stimuli, Inc., to foster a greater synthesis between Black cultural expression and European American worship traditions. He noted that this synthesis would require Black Catholics to come to know and cherish their cultural tradition. Only then could they recognize that its vitality and dynamism can "enrich Christian and other forms of worship not only for Blacks but for all religionists."[26]

The 1970s: Flowering of the Black Catholic Liturgical Movement

The aftermath of the Civil Rights movement left many of the one million Black Catholics in the United States eager for change. The organization of Black Catholic

---

21. Copeland, "African American Catholics," 103; Clarence R. J. Rivers, "Thank God We Ain't What We Was: The State of the Liturgy in the Black Catholic Community," in *Theology: A Portrait in Black*, ed. Thaddeus Posey, O.F.M. Cap. (Pittsburgh: Capuchin Press, 1980), 68–70. See also Sharpes, "Black Catholic Gifts."

22. The following year he received national recognition when his composition, "God is Love," was performed at the Liturgical Conference in St. Louis, Mo. during the first Mass celebrated completely in English in the United States.

23. Sharpes, "Black Catholic Gifts," 49–50.

24. Copeland, "African American Catholics," 103.

25. Clarence R. J. Rivers, *Soulfull Worship* (Washington, D.C.: National Office for Black Catholics, 1974), 14.

26. Clarence R. J. Rivers, *The Spirit in Worship* (Cincinnati: Stimuli, 1978). See also Clarence R. J. Rivers, "Music and the Liberation of Black Catholics," *Freeing the Spirit* 1, no. 1 (1971): 26–28.

leadership, begun during the 1960s, culminated in the founding of a National Office for Black Catholics (NOBC) in 1970.[27] The same year, the First National Black Lay Catholic Caucus was held, focusing the lay leadership of Black Catholics on a national level once again. The 1970s saw the naming of four Black bishops in key cities who began to shape an episcopal presence that would take eloquent leadership in the 1980s.[28] Theologians began to formulate a Black Catholic theology, adding their voices to the significant work on Black theology already written by their Protestant brothers and sisters. Historians retraced the evolution of Black Catholics, providing first access to the strong, if often invisible, presence of African Americans Catholics in the United States. Together, these leaders precipitated what has aptly been called the "Black Catholic Movement" of the 1970s.[29]

In this context, the American Church saw a flowering of the Black Catholic liturgical movement launched by Clarence Rivers in the 1960s. In 1970, Rivers became the first director of the NOBC's Department of Culture and Worship. Through workshops, conferences, and publications, this department began to create a platform for a true indigenization of Black Catholic worship.[30] Under its auspices, the journal *Freeing the Spirit* was launched as a forum for exploring issues pertinent to Black worship and as a means of providing liturgical resources, images of African art, and newly composed music to pastoral leaders. Black liturgists, composers, and musicians were enlisted to offer workshops on Catholic liturgy around the country. The primary goal of these workshops was to educate and "liberate" Black Catholics to reclaim the fullness of their religious and ritual heritage and to train ministers for the tasks of leadership. These gatherings enabled composers and musicians to explore various styles of Black sacred music and to collaborate in the creation of new musical settings. Composers Grayson Brown, Robert Ray, Rawn Harbor, and others took up the work of blending the idioms of jazz, gospel, and soul with European musical styles to create a new synthesis: the beginnings of a Black Catholic liturgical repertoire. In the process, Clarence Rivers encouraged musicians to be "free to use traditional 'Catholic' musics and allow them free interplay with our Afro-American musics. . . . Like our forefathers who combined African and white Protestant music to produce the rich musics of Black America, musically liberated Black Catholics . . . [will bring a] still greater enrichment to the Afro-American [musical] styles, [a] further originality."[31]

As the leadership articulated the path of liturgical indigenization, Black Catholic renewal began to flourish in pockets around the country. Beginning in the late 1960s,

---

27. The NOBC, with the endorsement of the Bishops' Conference of the United States, functioned as an umbrella organization to focus attempts to make the Church relevant to the needs of the Black community.

28. Joseph Lawson Howze; Eugene Antonio Marino, S.S.J.; Joseph Francis, S.V.D.; and James Patterson Lyke, O.F.M. were ordained auxiliary bishops of Natchez-Jackson, Miss., Washington, D.C., Newark, N.J., and Cleveland, Ohio respectively. Howze was named bishop of Biloxi, Miss. in 1977, becoming the first Black ordinary in the United States since 1900.

29. See Sharpes, "Black Catholic Gifts."

30. Copeland, "African American Catholics," 104.

31. Rivers, "Music and the Liberation of Black Catholics," 28.

some predominantly Black parishes had taken initiatives to incorporate African American music, artistic expression, and modes of participation in their worship.[32] "Black Catholics," wrote M. Shawn Copeland, "dove into the treasure chest of African American sacred music, lifting up the spirituals, plundering the Baptist hymnal, tracking down organists competent in the Black musical genre and idiom—often from the Baptist congregation across town!"[33] Gospel choirs were formed in several urban parishes around the country. Drums, pianos, and other instruments found a new home in Catholic worship spaces. The first Black lay deacons were trained to add a Black liturgical presence in parishes with White clerical leadership.[34] Liturgical vestments and altar coverings were created in African styles and fabrics. Statuary was replaced with images of African saints. The liberation colors—red, black, and green—used by Black Americans in the past and revived during the Civil Rights movement, appeared in Catholic churches. This "reclothing" of church and ministers allowed Black Catholics to say in a new way, "We are here, and we're going to make this Church our home." But not all Black Catholics responded positively to these directions. Resistance due to Catholic training and a diversity of perspectives signaled a truth that would become clearer in the 1980s: Black culture is not monolithic, but diverse and dynamic.

Black Catholic Liturgical Music

It is not surprising that music was an early focus of parish renewal. Black sacred song is perhaps the most comprehensive repository of Black spirituality, theology, and cosmology. Spirituals were the first form of African American music to be used by Catholic communities, providing a cultural touchstone that reached back into the roots and early manifestations of Black religious experience in the United States.[35] As Thea Bowman—scholar, musician, poet, and educator—noted:

> African Americans in sacred song preserved the memory of African religious rites and symbols, of a holistic African spirituality, of rhythms and tones and harmonies that communicated their deepest feelings across barriers of region and language. African Americans in fields and quarters, at work, in secret meetings, in slave festivals, in churches, camp meets and revivals, wherever they met or congregated, consoled and strengthened themselves and one another with sacred song—moans, chants, shouts, psalms, hymns,

---

32. Leon C. Roberts, "The Development of African American Liturgical Music Since Vatican II," in *Our Roots and Gifts* (Washington, D.C.: Archdiocese of Washington, 1989), 30.

33. Copeland, "African American Catholics," 103.

34. Copeland, "African American Catholics," 105–106. Copeland cites a pastoral training program begun in Detroit in the late '60s to provide Black men with the theological, spiritual, and personal formation necessary to function in the Black community as lay or nonordained ministers.

35. Roberts, "Development of African American Liturgical Music," 29; Jacqueline Cogdell Dje Dje, "An Expression of Black Identity: The Use of Gospel Music in a Los Angeles Catholic Church," *Western Journal of Black Studies* 7, no. 3 (1983): 153.

and jubilees, first African songs, then African American songs. In the crucible of separation and suffering, African American sacred song was formed.[36]

The Biblical character of many spirituals made them a desirable expression of Black Catholic worship.[37] Many give voice to a "mystical identification with Jesus, with God, and all the heroes of the Hebrew and Christian scriptures."[38] Spirituals are expressions of faith with strong social implications. Created within a slave environment, they express a longing for radical change, for a freedom and deliverance that the power of God in Jesus can bring about.[39]

Beginning in the 1970s, African American gospel music took on new importance for Catholic communities.[40] Gospel music carries a significantly different meaning than spirituals in Black culture. Spirituals grew out of a rural, Southern, slave environment and carry the affective emotions associated with that experience. Gospel music is rooted in the post–World War I migrations of African Americans from rural settings in the South to urban centers in the north and in the changing religious ideals that grew from this new sociological environment.[41] Jacqueline Dje Dje proposed that gospel music's reflection of the sensibilities of Blacks in urban areas gives it a particular attraction for some Catholic communities, since "Catholicism in the United States has essentially been an urban phenomenon."[42]

Catholic musicians drew on other repertoires of Black sacred music as well. Hymnody formerly adopted by the Black church, especially those hymns beloved of African American communities such as "Blessed Assurance" and "Amazing Grace," were incorporated into Catholic worship. As in Black church contexts, Catholic musicians performed these hymns according to Black aesthetic sensitivities, adopting a performance practice that required improvisation, embellishment, and the dynamic

---

36. Celestine Cepress, *Sister Thea Bowman, Shooting Star: Selected Writings and Speeches*. (Winona, Minn.: St. Mary's Press, Christian Brothers Publications, 1985), 59–60.

37. National Conference of Catholic Bishops, Secretariat for Black Catholics, and Secretariat for the Liturgy, *Plenty Good Room: The Spirit and Truth of African American Catholic Worship* (Washington, D.C.: USCC Publishing Office, 1990), nos. 61–62; Cepress, *Sister Thea Bowman,* 64; Wyatt Tee Walker, *The Soul of Black Worship* (New York: Martin Luther King Fellows Press, 1984), 56; Wyatt Tee Walker, *"Somebody's Calling My Name": Black Sacred Music and Social Change* (Valley Forge, Pa.: Judson Press, 1979), 52–54.

38. Joseph A. Brown, "Theological Themes within African American Religious Experience." Paper presented at the Conference on the Experience of African American Catholics in the Life of the Church, Annual Meeting of the African American Jesuits of the United States, Jesuit School of Theology, Berkeley, Calif., 13 Oct. 1995. He highlighted this "mystical identification" as an important theological theme within African American religious experience.

39. Costen, *African American Christian Worship,* 96.

40. Dje Dje, "An Expression of Black Identity," 153.

41. Ibid. See also Jacqueline Cogdell Dje Dje, "Change and Differentiation: The Adoption of Black American Music in the Catholic Church," *Ethnomusicology* 30, no. 2 (1986): 223–252; Mellonee Burnim, "The Black Gospel Music Tradition: A Complex of Ideology, Aesthetic, and Behavior," in *More Than Dancing,* ed. Irene V. Jackson (Westport, Conn.: Greenwood Press, 1985), 149; Walker, *"Somebody's Calling My Name,"* 127–159.

42. Dje Dje, "An Expression of Black Identity," 153.

communication of "soul."[43] In the words of Clarence Rivers: "The essence of Black music is freedom. When music is free, it is soulful at its source, and soul-stirring in its effect."[44]

A Black Catholic Liturgical Aesthetic, Theology, and Spirituality

During the 1970s, Clarence Rivers continued his prophetic work of articulating a Black Catholic liturgical aesthetic. His 1974 *Soulfull Worship* mined the resources of Black worship for Catholics—the importance of the spoken word, music, dance, and drama; the centrality of the congregation; and the key role of the pastor. His second publication, *The Spirit in Worship* (1978), pushed deeper for a true integration of Black culture and Catholic worship. Identifying the African roots of Black worship, Rivers articulated the centrality of "soul" in the Black religious aesthetic. He contended that for worship to satisfy the religious longings of Black Catholics, this quality of "soul" must permeate the entire ritual event—its prayer styles, preaching, and sacramental action. Rivers contrasted the oral/aural, poetic, and holistic predilections of African cultures with the more "ocular," print-oriented, and linear orientations of Western cultures that have shaped the patterns of Catholic worship, demonstrating how the latter mitigates against "soulful" worship.[45]

Liturgical renewal during this period was inseparable from the work of many scholars to retrieve the history of Black Catholics in the United States and to articulate the theology and spirituality implicit in their ethno-religious heritage.[46] In 1977, the NOBC sponsored a national ecumenical conference on worship and spirituality in the Black community that culminated in the publication of *This Far by Faith: American Black Worship and its African Roots*. Cyprian Rowe, addressing the symposium, signaled a critical theme: the need to acknowledge the "distinctiveness of Black culture."[47] Rowe stated that the distinctiveness of Black culture is most evident in those "areas of Afro-American life that Euro-Americans were not interested in . . . music and art and church. Those were particular worlds in which [Black] people were not compelled by circumstances to interact constantly with European culture."[48] Likewise, theologian William B. McClain pointed to the centrality of worship in the formation of Black spirituality and theology.[49] The most distinctive element of Black worship, he contended, is its ability to discern and celebrate the presence, power, and victory of God within the pain, struggles, and injustices of Black life. Black worship symbolizes the inherent worth and worthiness of God's Black creation and celebrates their God-given power to

---

43. See Walker, *"Somebody's Calling My Name."*
44. Rivers, *Soulfull Worship*, 42.
45. Rivers, *The Spirit in Worship,* 15–48.
46. See, for example, Albert J. Raboteau, *Slave Religion* (New York: Oxford University Press, 1978).
47. Rowe, "The Case for a Distinctive Black Culture," 20–27.
48. Ibid., 23.
49. McClain, "Black Religious Experience," 29–37. What follows is summarized from this source.

survive and succeed. But, McClain asserted, all aspects of Black worship must speak of people's real concerns. Black worship must speak to a people who, in the midst of oppression, pursue liberation, wholeness, and holiness, trusting Jesus, the Emancipator, to be companion and guide.

A third conference participant, Bishop James Lyke, addressed the application of Black cultural considerations to Catholic worship.[50] Lyke maintained that this process must be carried out primarily on the level of local pastoral ministry, with real people, real congregations, and real life. This requires

> a certain inevitable and necessary tension: tension between the charism of leadership and the charism of the people; liturgically, tension between what is given us as guidelines, directives, books, and what the local church discovers in applying them. It is . . . impossible for an official Vatican agency serving hundreds of millions of people all over the world to answer the needs of every cultural and subcultural group. That is what pastoral ministry is for.[51]

Lyke explored the challenges of his own liturgical ministry in the Black Catholic community—the importance of discovering authentic feasts and festivals that celebrate Black experience and the challenge of creating a worship environment that reflects the beauty and history of Black people created in the image of God. He stressed that the vitality of African and African American cultural values, honored in the liturgy, must overflow into the whole life of parish and society. "There is no conflict, no contradiction between being Black and being Catholic," Lyke stated. "Quite the contrary. One does a disservice to the church if one is in the Roman Catholic community and if one is not, at the same time, as Black as one can be."[52]

In 1978, the first Black Catholic Theology Symposium was held in Baltimore. Thirty-three participants addressed a broad range of issues: Black values and self-concept, an African-based spirituality, and directions for catechetics and pastoral theology. In this context, liturgists Glen V. Jeanmarie and Clarence Rivers reiterated that "the whole range of Black culture [must be brought] to bear on our worship efforts."[53] Expressive prayer, vibrant preaching, and spirited singing cannot be isolated insertions but are part of a transformation of the whole symbol system of Catholic worship. Jeanmarie challenged Church authority to allow the composition of new eucharistic prayer texts that "flow from the prayer tradition of Black Folks."[54] Rivers charged Black leaders to develop programs to train Black liturgical ministers, musicians, prayer leaders, and preachers; to educate people to a deeper understanding of

---

50. James P. Lyke, "Application of Black Cultural Considerations to Catholic Worship," in *This Far By Faith: American Black Worship and Its African Roots,* ed. National Office for Black Catholics (Washington, D.C.: Liturgical Conference, 1977), 50–57.

51. Ibid., 57.

52. Ibid., 54–55.

53. Rivers, "Thank God We Ain't What We Was," 70. See also Jeanmarie, "Black Catholic Worship."

54. Jeanmarie, "Black Catholic Worship," 85.

worship; and to sustain and challenge parishes where Black culture had already been welcomed lest they become "inauthentically Catholic in their scope while becoming authentically Black."[55] He called for increased cultural interchange with the Church in the Caribbean, Latin America, and "Mother Africa." But Rivers also noted a growing ecclesiastical racist backlash that threatened to impede the progress already made. In a bold but truthful statement, Rivers claimed that the full recovery of Black spirituality and culture in Catholic liturgy is not only a matter of aesthetics—it is a work of justice. "To consider the problem of Black culture within the Catholic Church as merely or even primarily a question of aesthetic preference is a failure to understand history."[56]

A Black Catholic Rite?

Within the climate of the Black Catholic movement of the '70s, the first questions were raised about the desirability of a separate liturgical rite, even a separate church, for Catholics of African descent in the United States. For some, separation seemed the only way to avoid a persistent "White bias" in decisions regarding Catholic life and worship. The NOBC had been founded in 1970 to enable the Church "to meet the needs of Black people as a people of dignity," recognizing that their needs are distinct from those of the White Catholic community.[57] A breaking away of Black Catholics was not intended but rather a "'functional separatism' with the ultimate objective of integration" in the larger Church. That same year, A. Donald Bourgeois, professor at Ohio State University, addressing a Black Catholic lay congress, "called for a doctrinally orthodox church injected 'with meaning and hope and common life' that would have special relevance for Blacks."[58] The following year, the National Black Catholic Clergy Caucus (NBCCC) announced that it would study the potential of an African American rite within the Catholic Church. However, these ideas were opposed as "divisive and harmful" by Auxiliary Bishop Harold Perry of New Orleans, who was then the only Black bishop in the United States, and Emmanuel K. Nsubuga, a Ugandan Prelate visiting the United States.[59] The question would resurface in the 1980s as pastoral leaders struggled to find ways to release the fullness of Black giftedness within the American Church.

As the 1970s concluded, significant changes were visible in the life and worship of African American Catholics. Yet in spite of many gains, racism persisted within Church life. The American hierarchy had yet to lend major support to the efforts of Black Catholic leaders. At the prompting of the "Call to Action" meeting in Detroit, and with the renewed insistence of Black leadership organizations, the U.S. Catholic bishops issued their second pastoral letter on racism in 1979, entitled *Brothers and Sisters to Us All*. "Racism is an evil which endures in our society and in our Church,"

---

55. Rivers, "Thank God We Ain't What We Was," 73.
56. Ibid., 68.
57. Sharpes, "Black Catholic Gifts," 29.
58. Ibid., 29, quoting the *Buffalo Magnificat.*
59. Ibid., 30, quoting the *Michigan Catholic.*

they claimed. But "there must be no turning back along the road of justice, no sighing for bygone times of privilege, no nostalgia for simple solutions from another age."[60]

The 1980s: African American Catholic Liturgy, "Authentically Black and Truly Catholic"

As the 1980s dawned, Black Catholics were poised to claim a new synthesis of their Black and Catholic heritages. But the '80s would also be a time of wrestling with deeper issues of identity, leadership, differentiation, self-determination, and power. All of this had an impact on the development of African American liturgy. In 1984, the Black bishops called upon the 1.3 million Black Catholics to share their "precious gifts of Blackness" with the larger American Church. They articulated a direction for liturgical renewal—"authentically Black and truly Catholic."[61] Eight new Black bishops[62] were named during this decade, and Bishop Eugene Marino was made the first Black archbishop in the United States. Working together, these bishops become a catalyst within the National Conference of Catholic Bishops for the creation of several national secretariats to address the pressing pastoral and liturgical needs of Black Catholics. In 1987, the first National Black Catholic Congress of the twentieth century met to develop a National Pastoral Plan for evangelization. This plan gained the approval of the American bishops in 1989. Throughout the 1980s, historians and theologians continued to develop resources for a deeper self-understanding and self-determination on the part of Black Catholics, but this same decade would see the first dramatic split within the Black Catholic community. In 1989, Rev. George Stallings founded the African American Catholic Community, centered at the Imani Temple in Washington, D.C. His purpose was to "give Black Catholics total control over their faith" and to develop a liturgical rite that reflected their culture and history. His actions raised, and continue to raise, questions about the full implications of the processes of inculturation undertaken by Black Catholics.

What We Have Seen and Heard: *A Liturgical Agenda for the 1980s*

In 1984, ten Black bishops issued their first pastoral letter, *What We Have Seen and Heard* (*WWSH*). The primary focus of the letter was evangelization, a work that must

---

60. National Conference of Catholic Bishops, *Brothers and Sisters to Us All. U.S. Bishops' Pastoral Letter on Racism in Our Day* (Washington, D.C.: USCC Publishing Office, 1979), nos, 1 and 14. Ironically, the title indicates the centrality of White membership to Catholic life.

61. Black Catholic Bishops of the United States, *Brothers and Sisters,* 31.

62. The new bishops were Emerson Moore (Auxiliary of New York, N.Y.); Moses Bosco Anderson, S.S.E. (auxiliary of Detroit, Mich.); Wilton Daniel Gregory (auxiliary of Chicago, Ill.); James Terry Steib, S.V.D. (auxiliary of St. Louis, Mo.); John Houston Ricard, S.S.J. (auxiliary of Baltimore, Md.); Carl A. Fisher, S.S.J. (auxiliary of Los Angeles, Calif.); Curtis J. Gillory, S.V.D. (auxiliary of Galveston-Houston, Tex.); and Leonard Olivier, S.V.D. (auxiliary of Washington, D.C.).

be grounded in the socio-cultural and spiritual distinctiveness of the Black community and engage all its members. The bishops contended that liturgy is an essential aspect of evangelization—a primary place for Black believers to discover a "homeland" in the Catholic Church. For this to happen, liturgical celebrations must become a "more intense expression of the spiritual vitality of those who are of African origin."[63] Liturgy in the Black community must be at once "authentically Black and truly Catholic." To be authentically Black, worship must utilize the distinctive Black cultural idiom: in music, preaching, bodily expression, artistic furnishing, vestments, and in the whole tempo of worship. It must release the power of "Black Spirituality," a spiritual heritage rooted in an African past. The bishops identify four major characteristics of Black spirituality: it is *contemplative*, sensing "the awe of God's transcendence and the vital intimacy of his closeness"; it is *holistic*, embracing "intellect and emotion, spirit and body, action and contemplation, individual and community, sacred and secular"; it is *joyful*, expressed through "movement and song, rhythm and feeling, color and sensation, exultation and thanksgiving"; and finally, it is *communitarian*, assuming that "the 'I' takes its meaning in the 'we'" and finds its call to holiness within the social body. The bishops contend that a rich expression of this Black spirituality is possible within the shape of the revised Roman liturgy, but they caution that vibrant preaching and music, the caché of the Black religious heritage, must never "overwhelm the liturgy as a balanced unified action." Rather it should "invite the worshiping community to a more profound participation in the total sacramental experience."[64] The bishops commend Black liturgists, artists, composers, and musicians who have "tirelessly presented workshops and conferences on Black liturgical expression" and call for continued collaborative work that will release "our rich gifts of Blackness for the whole church."[65]

The State of Black Catholic Liturgy: Bishop James Lyke's Survey

A year before the release of *WWSH*, James Lyke, one of the bishops who issued the document, conducted a survey of twenty-seven Black leaders in an attempt to assess the state of Black Catholic liturgy in the United States.[66] Based on their pastoral experience, twenty-five respondents to the survey identified indigenous music and dynamic preaching as the "essential elements of liturgical expression for Black communities." They affirmed that lively participation, fellowship, freedom of expression, spontaneity of prayer styles, and animated, indigenous leadership were critical as well. However, when questioned if the "present Roman Rite constrains liturgical expression in the

---

63. Black Catholic Bishops of the United States, *Brothers and Sisters,* 30. What follows is taken from pages 8, 30–32.

64. The vision of worship elucidated in this document lacks the breadth articulated by Clarence Rivers a decade earlier. It also does not explicitly elaborate how the Black religious heritage might "overwhelm" the liturgy, or what is perceived as "a balanced unified action."

65. Black Catholic Bishops of the United States, *Brothers and Sisters,* 32.

66. James P. Lyke, "Liturgical Expression in the Black Community," *Worship* 57, no. 1 (1983): 14–33. What follows summarizes key aspects of this survey.

Fr. Clarence Rivers (left) and Eddie Bonnomere receiving awards for their leadership at a National Office for Black Catholics Liturgy Workshop in the late 1970s. (Courtesy of Fr. James Pawlicki, S.V.D., Bay St. Louis, Mississippi, photographer.)

Black community," fifteen of these pastoral leaders answered with a strong "yes," in clear contrast to the conclusions drawn in *WWSH*. The remaining ten felt that the current rite allowed for sufficient balance and freedom. All agreed that spontaneity and emotive expression embodied the genius of Black people and were essential to the experience of an "adequately enacted ritual," but some voiced caution lest these dynamic factors "obscure the sense of mystery and symbolism in the liturgy." Thus they signaled an issue that would face Black pastoral leaders well into the future: Which takes precedence, the indigenous sense of Black expressive worship or the currently prescribed structures of Roman Catholic liturgy?

Bishop Lyke offers four observations about the survey's findings. First, he notes a continuing tension as to whether emotion or intellect, heart or mind will dominate Black Catholic worship. Second, he acknowledges that Black Catholics are quite diverse, and no single model of liturgy will satisfy all. Third, two key areas of debate remain: how to be "Catholic" in the selection of liturgical music, and how to be effective in the employment of preaching styles. Finally, Lyke cautions that much attention is still needed toward the whole "environment" within which Black Catholics worship—the action, the symbols, the liturgical feasts, the heroes and heroines upheld, and perhaps most importantly, the "psychologically oppressive" effect of many church buildings that remain "clothed" in the cultural expressions of other ethnic communities for whom they were built.

Fire in the Pews: *A Portrait of Worship and Music in Black Catholic Parishes*

In 1987, a documentary on Black Catholic worship entitled *Fire in the Pews* was released.[67] The film focuses on the experience of twelve predominantly Black parishes in eight cities around the country.[68] It includes interviews with parishioners, clergy, and other Black Catholic leaders. The viewer is immediately struck by the abundant display of vital and energized worship, the engaging and powerful styles of preaching, and the richly orchestrated, dynamic, and participatory music performed with a sense of "communal passion." The pastor of St. Augustine's in Washington, D.C. attributes this vibrancy to a renewal that flourished in the Black Catholic community in the decade preceding the filming, a renewal signaled by an almost tripling of the membership of St. Augustine's. Members of several parishes comment on the importance of finding a "home" in the Church: a place where they can express their Catholic faith in worship that is free, personal, affective, and full of warmth; that provides "a more outward expression of how the Lord touches us"; that is connected with real life situations; and that gives people energy for building the Kingdom. They speak of the importance of being able to express their joys, struggles, and even weaknesses, "because that's where the healing is."

Blacks are attracted to Catholic worship "because of its structure, rubrics, solemnity, pageantry, pomp, and circumstance," comments Rev. George Stallings, a priest in the archdiocese of Washington, D.C.[69] "We are a theatrical people. . . . Catholic liturgy is drama, it is entertainment, in the holistic sense of entertainment . . . involving the senses, smell, the incense, the eyes, the costumes, the music, the touch, the 'Bread of Life' and the 'Cup of Salvation,'. . . the feel that you get, the embrace." At the same time, Black Catholics bring to Catholic liturgy unique and powerful gifts—among them "our unique ability to break the Word and to savor that Word within the arms of a loving community."[70] In the words of Thea Bowman:

---

67. A subsequent edition of the film was edited to eliminate scenes of George Stallings after his formation of Imani Temple.

68. The parishes were St. Augustine's in Washington, D.C.; St. Francis de Sales, St. Monica's, and Xavier University in New Orleans, La.; St. Teresa's and Holy Guardian Angels in St. Louis, Mo.; St. Mark's and St. Aloysius in Harlem, N.Y.; Holy Child Jesus in Caton, Miss.; St. Sabina in Chicago, Ill.; Our Lady of Charity in Brooklyn, N.Y.; and Sacred Heart in Queens, N.Y. The most extensive coverage was given to St. Augustine's parish.

69. George Stallings was then the director of a newly established Office of Evangelization for the Archdiocese of Washington, D.C. The insights he brought to this documentary reiterate a liturgical theology that Clarence Rivers articulated in the 1970s and 1980s and situated Stallings at the heart of Black Catholic leadership in the 1980s.

70. Thea Bowman, *Fire in the Pews.*

Black people from Africa are people of the Word. Among us the Word is celebrated, it is incarnate, it is embodied in song, in dance, in story, in poetry, in sculpture, in relationships. What you witness in our churches is that embodiment and that celebration of the Word.[71]

Stallings goes on to remark that preaching in the Black community is heavily rooted in the Word of God and in the experience of Black people.

[Preaching] has to touch the fiber of one's being in order to be effective and in order to bring forth an affective response. . . . If people are going to be fired up to do something for God, they have to feel the power of that Word. The problem in many of our churches is that we have churches that are not on fire with the word of God. . . . You cannot have fire in the pews if there is ice in the pulpit![72]

One of the striking aspects of *Fire in the Pews* is the response (both enacted and verbalized) of many White Catholics who choose to participate in African American parish life and worship. "The Black church has gifts the white church is hungry for," comments Rev. Michael Phleger, white pastor of St. Sabina's in Chicago. Others echo these sentiments: "People are looking for more than what is being given. I firmly believe the Black Catholic Community will be the salvation of the Catholic Church in America."[73]

Black Episcopal Leadership and the Creation of National Offices

The national impact of Black episcopal leadership continued to increase during the 1980s. In 1984, Black bishops received approval for a Black Liturgy Subcommittee within the National Conference of Catholic Bishops (NCCB). Two years later the NCCB, in response to the continued call of Black bishops to provide "an effective national structure for the support of Black Catholics,"[74] established a Standing Committee for Black Catholics. This was followed in 1988 by the creation of a permanent Secretariat for Black Catholics within the NCCB.[75] The creation of this secretariat was perceived as "a sign of the respect from the hierarchy for the potential of Black Catholics and . . . a particular mark of respect for the Black Catholic bishops who played a major role in obtaining this office."[76]

---

71. Thea Bowman, *Fire in the Pews*.

72. George Stallings, *Fire in the Pews*.

73. Ibid.

74. Ronald L. Sharpes, "Black Catholics in the United States: A Historical Chronology," *U.S. Catholic Historian* 12, no. 1 (1994): 138. It is important to note that Black Catholic leaders originally decided not to place the NOBC under the auspices of the NCCB. In the 1980s they reversed this decision to establish definitive ties with the bishops' conference, believing that fuller recognition was now possible and that Black bishops could expand the boundaries of episcopal decision makers.

75. Sharpes, "Black Catholic Gifts," 53. The Secretariat for Black Catholics was renamed the Secretariat for African American Catholics in 1991.

76. Copeland, "African American Catholics," 112.

The Subcommittee on Black Worship, chaired by Bishop Wilton Gregory, working with the Bishops' Committee on the Liturgy, began to address questions of liturgical inculturation and to articulate guidelines for the celebration of Eucharist. These efforts culminated in the NCCB's publication of *In Spirit and Truth: Black Catholic Reflections on the Order of Mass* (1987).[77] In light of the bishops' liturgical agenda, "authentically Black and truly Catholic," *In Spirit and Truth* focuses primarily on the latter portion of that ideal—truly Catholic. It begins with the revised "Order of Mass," the "General Instruction on the Roman Missal," and other related documents assessing how Black Catholics might "utilize fully all the present options [within the revised rite] to bring our cultural treasures to the worship life of the Church we love."[78] Each item of the order of Mass is carefully laid out, with remarks about what options are permitted and comments regarding what might interfere with the flow of the ritual action. Despite the cautious tone of the document, it concludes with a remarkable statement:

> Like all Catholics, Black Catholics are still experiencing the richness of the renewed liturgy. They have been heartened to witness so many creative and inspiring celebrations of the Church's liturgy. *As they continue to probe the possibilities inherent in the Roman liturgy, they will recognize its limitations as well as its still untapped potential.*[79]

Three years later, the Secretariat for Black Catholics, in conjunction with the NCCB, stated that while *In Spirit and Truth* "provides an excellent model and serves as a worthy signpost," it does not exhaust the requirements of a full inculturation of Black culture in Catholic worship. "African American Catholics are in the process of developing and continuing a tradition"; this process requires serious exploration of "the genuine and authentic African heritage that is ours" and "the powerful gifts of African American culture."[80]

In 1983, the Black Catholic Clergy Conference inaugurated a project to assemble the first Black Catholic hymnal in the United States.[81] Black Catholic composers Rawn Harbor and Leon Roberts, in conjunction with Marjorie Gabriel-Burrow, were invited to collaborate in the study, selection, composition, and arrangement of hymns and service music for the new hymnal. In 1987, *Lead Me, Guide Me* was published. M. Shawn Copeland, assessing the impact of the hymnal, speaks of it as "thoroughly Black and thoroughly Catholic." She concludes that in juxtaposing several traditions—spirituals, gospel, Gregorian plain chant, Black arrangements of Dr. Watts' style hymns, as well

---

77. National Conference of Catholic Bishops, Secretariat for the Liturgy, and Black Liturgy Subcommittee, *In Spirit and Truth: Black Catholic Reflections on the Order of Mass* (Washington, D.C.; USCC Publishing Office, 1987). An earlier form of this document, prepared by Black leaders, called for more self-determination and ongoing experimentation. However, this was rejected because it was perceived by the drafters of *In Spirit and Truth* that the time of post–Vatican II experimentation had ended.

78. Ibid., 2.

79. Ibid., 28. Italics ours.

80. *Plenty Good Room*, nos. 123, 124.

81. Numerous persons were engaged in this process, including representatives of various Black Catholic Organizations. See Preface to *Lead Me, Guide Me* (Chicago: GIA Publications, Inc., 1987), 1.

as Catholic standards and new African American Catholic compositions—the hymnal "recognizes and affirms both the commonality and plurality of Black Catholic experience . . . [and serves as] a sign of some maturity in this long period of indigenization."[82]

Continued Questions Regarding the Full Implications of Liturgical Inculturation

Together with liturgical renewal, education, evangelization, and catechesis were among the strongest focuses of Black Catholic leadership throughout the '80s. Scholars and pastoral leaders Toinette Eugene, Nathan Jones, Eva Marie Lumas, and Bishop James Lyke, to name but a few, developed approaches to evangelization and catechesis that took Black theology and Black experience as starting points and that remained "faithful to both our heritages."[83] Together, they sought to develop a type of catechesis that "offers a liberating experience of religion, faith, and religious education for the whole person, rooted in, attentive and faithful to the common and plural Black Catholic experience." They underscored the truth that revelation for Black persons begins precisely in the Black experience, an awareness that would be articulated as "Africentric" in the 1990s. They recognized that African and African American folklore, music, poetry, and art are carriers of deep religious truth and sensitivity, and that the history, theology, and religious traditions of Black people need to interact with Catholic doctrine in vital and dynamic ways. This work on evangelization and catechesis posed new questions about the full implications of liturgical inculturation in the Black community and focused discontent with processes of "adaptation" that were still experienced as superficial. How will liturgical prayers have power within the Black community if they do not capture the modes of speaking, the turns of phrase, the aphorisms, and the proverbs that are bearers of truth in an oral/aural culture? If language, music, dance, and art are carriers of revelation, are they not essential rather than peripheral to the liturgical action? And how can preaching name the action of God in the community if it is not rooted in Black experience, the primary place of God's revelation for the African American Catholic community?

Implications of Ongoing Inculturation: An African American Liturgical Rite?

Questions regarding the desirability of a separate liturgical rite, even a separate church, for Catholics of African descent in the United States that had been dismissed in the 1970s as "divisive and harmful" resurfaced in the late 1980s. During the 1987 National Black Catholic Congress in Washington, D.C., a small group of the delegates attempted to present a proposal for the development of an African American liturgical

---

82. Copeland, "African American Catholics," 105. A differing perception of the editorial process is offered by some on the editorial board who felt that decisions about which songs to include did not totally reflect the choice of the hymnal's Black editors.

83. Copeland, "African American Catholics," 105–107. What follows, including quotes, draws on this source.

rite. However, the congress' internal polity kept the topic from being placed on the agenda.[84] Within a month of the national congress, Pope John Paul II spoke to an audience of Black Catholic leaders in New Orleans. The pope reiterated the call for African Americans to present their "gift of Blackness to the Church," but he cautioned the participants:

> It is important to realize that there is no black church, no white church, no American church; but there is and must be in the one church of Jesus Christ, a home for blacks, whites, Americans, every culture and race.[85]

The pope's remarks did not resonate with the ethno-religious self-understanding that characterized the Black Catholic movement of the time. Giles Conwill, a Black Catholic cultural anthropologist, captured the mood of the movement by saying that African American Catholics had begun to speak of their religious specificity as "Black Catholicism" rather than the "Catholicism of Blacks."[86] Conwill described the shift in language as an indication that Black Catholics had moved beyond the Eurocentric confines of the faith they had inherited. They had arrived at "a condition of true indigenization, with Black leadership; a deep, abiding, rooted, and flourishing identity."[87] Nonetheless, their full membership in the Catholic Church remained an elusive goal. In 1989, Sister Thea Bowman addressed the American Catholic bishops:

> Surviving our history, physically, mentally, emotionally, morally, spiritually, faithfully, and joyfully, our people developed a culture that was African and American, that was formed and enriched by all that we experienced. And despite all this, despite the civil rights movement in the '60s and the socio-educational gains of the '70s, Blacks in the 1980s are still struggling . . . *still trying to find a home in the homeland and a home in the [Catholic] church.*[88]

The Right to Rites

That same year, moved by the struggle "to find a home in the church," Rev. George Stallings founded Imani Temple—a separate Black but Catholic church of which he

---

84. The proposal was initiated by Fr. Al McKnight, C.P.P.S., a member of the NBCCC. The congress trustees excluded the proposal from the agenda on the grounds that the issue had not been raised within the (arch)diocesan reflection days, which surfaced the "major topics" for consideration by the congress delegates. Apropos to this, the only way to get the proposal on the agenda was to have fifty percent plus one of the delegates sign a petition requesting that the proposal be raised from the floor. This required the petition to be circulated, signed, and submitted to the trustees within twenty-four hours. Supporters of the initiative deemed the task to be impossible and abandoned the effort.

85. Pope John Paul II, "The Pope's Address to Black Catholics," 252.

86. See Giles Conwill, "The Word Becomes Black Flesh," in *Evangelizing Blacks,* ed. Glenn C. Smith (New York: Paulist Press, 1988), 58.

87. Ibid.

88. Thea Bowman, "To Be Black and Catholic," *Origins* 19, no. 8 (July 1989): 115. Italics ours.

later became archbishop. He argued that for African Americans to fully express their culture and history in Catholic worship, they needed a specific rite distinct from the Latin rite of the Roman Catholic Church.[89] Therefore, he adopted an unofficial English-language version of a liturgical rite approved by the Vatican for use in the African nation of Zaire.[90] While Stallings' action in creating a separate church was criticized by many Black Catholics,[91] the question of a more radical adaptation of the Roman Catholic liturgy was being addressed by Black Catholic leaders. In the summer of 1989, the Joint Conference of Black Catholic Clergy, Sisters, and Seminarians invited Stallings to explain his actions at their annual convocation. After a lengthy and animated discussion, the conference decided to write Stallings' archbishop in support of Imani Temple, and two Black bishops offered to be "episcopal advisors" to the venture.[92] The joint conference also proposed that a study into the need for an African American Catholic rite be placed on the agenda of the 1992 National Black Catholic Congress.[93] What they envisioned was a canonically autonomous rite, involving both a unique liturgical rite and an autonomous structure of governance.[94] However, this direction was not embraced by all.

The most ardent opposition to an autonomous African American rite was articulated by D. Reginald Whitt, an African American Catholic priest and professor of canon law. Whitt identified several issues that supporters of the rite needed to address.[95] First, he questioned if the presence of African Americans in the Church was of sufficient duration, and their cultural-spiritual-religious patrimony of sufficient distinction, to warrant status with the twenty-three long-standing canonical rites that constitute the worldwide Catholic community. Second, he queried if autonomy from the Roman rite might relegate Black Catholics to "de facto second class" status and jeopardize their growing influence within the U.S. episcopacy and the larger Catholic Church. Whitt then asked if the limited financial resources and the relatively small number of priests and pastoral personnel available could adequately serve the more than two million African American Catholics and provide the necessary institutional infrastructure to meet their ministerial needs. Finally, he noted that affiliation with the Roman rite may be the most crucial factor that unifies U.S. Black Catholics and that the formulation of a new rite

---

89. Sharpes, "Black Catholic Gifts," 30–31.

90. D. R. Whitt, "Not Rite Now. An African-American Church?" *Church* (Spring 1990): 5–10.

91. Ibid.

92. National Black Sisters Conference (NBSC) Joint Conference Minutes, 1989. Stallings expressed his hope that Imani Temple would receive "de facto" approval from the U.S. National Conference of Catholic Bishops, and Bishops Terry Steib and Wilton Gregory volunteered to be episcopal advisors to the venture.

93. The national organizations endorsed the need and hope for Imani Temple to have full episcopal approbation for ministerial experimentation. Stallings' break from the Roman rite was the result of his renunciation of some essential Roman doctrines in 1990. No Black Catholic organization has supported Stallings' departure from orthodoxy.

94. NBSC Joint Conference Minutes, 1989.

95. See Whitt, "Not Rite Now." Even though the article was not published until 1990, it is reviewed here because it aptly captures the sentiments of those who opposed the proposal.

might jeopardize the ministerial needs of Blacks who choose to remain within the Roman Catholic Church. Whitt's passion and scholarship, used here to protest the formulation of an autonomous rite, would reappear in the mid-1990s, revealing a new appreciation of the African American community's ethno-religious patrimony. His energies and expertise would then be directed toward challenging the Church's resistance to formulating new liturgical structures for the African American Catholic community.

Theologian Edward Braxton tempered Whitt's somber evaluation while offering an alternative to the autonomous rite initiated by Stallings. He proposed the development of several "authorized liturgical models," paradigms, and examples that could be employed by communities to the extent they wish.[96] To develop these models, Braxton suggested that the American bishops seek approval from the Holy See for an extended period of careful experimentation and creative liturgical development. This would be carried out through the establishment of officially authorized centers for African American Catholic study in strategic places around the country. Here, pastors and scholars could gather examples of unofficial efforts to adapt the Roman rite for Black Catholic communities; establish a network of resource people—poets, musicians, artists, preachers, and fabric and vestment designers; determine places where African American Catholic worship had attained a level of excellence; and develop a range of liturgical services to be used on the parish level—bible services, liturgies of the word, revivals, and devotions to Mary and the saints. In conjunction with this work, Braxton proposed that several African American Catholics be invited to collaborate with the International Committee on English in the Liturgy (ICEL) in the creation of new eucharistic prayers that use the structure, language, and style of Black worship traditions while remaining faithful to Catholic beliefs. Despite the cogency of Braxton's proposals, no official action was taken.

As the 1980s drew to a close, questions of how to reconcile these varied pastoral and liturgical concerns remained a challenge. No matter what their position, most African American Catholics agreed that they had reached a crucial stage as a community. They now stood on the threshold of a new configuration of their faith and faithfulness. Whether or not there was a need for an African American canonical rite was yet to be decided. Only one thing was certain: they would fully participate in making the decision!

The 1990s: The Challenge of Inculturation and the Risk of Separation

Discussions of an African American rite gained momentum in the 1990s. A growing number of African American Catholics now questioned if the full expression of their faith required autonomy from the liturgical, if not the juridical, constraints of a Church that was ignorant of, or at least indifferent to, their specific cultural, spiritual, historical,

---

96. Braxton, "Sing America," 98–100.

and socio-political realities. In the early 1990s a second episcopal document on African American Catholic worship affirmed the distinct ethno-religious patrimony of the African American community and asserted its rightful place within Roman Catholicism. However, the document was criticized by many as too little too late. They insisted that the liturgical priorities of African American Catholics in the 1990s be guided by the theology of inculturation, the philosophy of Africentricity, and a reiteration of the pastoral need for indigenous leadership. Delegates to the 1992 National Black Catholic Congress affirmed these sentiments, voting for a nationwide opinion survey to assess the desirability of an African American Catholic rite. Although a majority of respondents to the survey rejected the idea of an autonomous canonical rite, they explicitly called for a fuller inclusion of African American culture within their celebration of the Roman rite. Even before the survey results were published in 1995, several significant liturgical innovations had been initiated. The 1990s witnessed the emergence of new and maturing pastoral leaders: five new African American bishops were appointed; four African American bishops were made ordinaries of a diocese; and one bishop became the vice-chairman (chair-elect) of the National Conference of Catholic Bishops. The number of African American Catholic theologians, scholars, administrators, and authors had tripled since the early 1980s. The 1990s, however, would also be marked by significant losses within the African American community: Thea Bowman, Bede Abram, James Lyke, Joseph Davis, Nathan Jones, Glenn Jeanmarie, Joseph Francis, Carl Fisher, and Leon Roberts died. Cyprian Rowe left the Catholic Church to join Imani Temple. Through it all, the liturgical insights and the diversity of African American Catholics became more focused. Issues that were raised in the previous three decades would resurface, but the nature of the inquiry would show greater depth, urgency, and conviction. (Cyprian Rowe recently returned to the Roman Catholic Church.)

Plenty Good Room

In 1990, the American bishops, with the Black Liturgy Subcommittee and the Bishops' Committee for Black Catholics, issued a second document, *Plenty Good Room: The Spirit and Truth of African American Catholic Worship.* In contrast to their earlier document, *In Spirit and Truth,* which focused primarily on how African American worship might be "truly Catholic," *Plenty Good Room* placed greater emphasis on the other side of the agenda: how it might be "authentically Black." The authors acknowledge that Black culture is not monolithic and that no single approach to liturgical expression will satisfy the religious longings of all African American Catholics. At the same time, they delineate certain dimensions of the culture that have had an impact on Black Catholic worship.[97] African American religious experience, they note, has been shaped by certain African perceptions: the all-pervasiveness of religion; a sense of the holy that encompasses the whole mystery of life; and an understanding of life as a total

---

97. The following images are drawn from *Plenty Good Room*, nos. 47–49, 85.

immersion in a sacred cosmos. These religious sensitivities have been honed within various Christian traditions, as well as the "church of the slave quarters and family gatherings where the spirituals were born, sung, danced, prayed, shouted, sermonized; where the sin-sick soul was healed."[98] The document reiterates that spirituality must be the starting point of a distinctively African American Catholic liturgy. In addition to the four dimensions of that spirituality articulated in *What We Have Seen and Heard*— contemplative, holistic, joyful, and communitarian—the document asserts that African American spirituality has a strongly intuitive and emotive base. For African Americans, emotion serves as a means of experiencing reality—a way of knowing and learning:

> African reason is more *logos* (word) than *ratio* (intellect). For *ratio* is compasses, square and sextant, scale and yardstick, whereas *logos* is living Word, the most specifically human expression of the neuro-sensorial impression. . . . The Black African *logos* in its ascent to the *Verbum* (transcendent) removes the rust from reality to bring out its primordial color, grain, texture, sound and color.[99]

This emotive way of knowing is not based primarily in the sense of sight, as in more *ocular*, printed-oriented Western cultures, but in the *oral, aural*, and *poetic* predilections of African cultures.[100] For this reason,

> there is a natural tendency for interpenetration and interplay, creating a concert or orchestration in which the ear sees, the eye hears, and where one both smells and tastes color, wherein all the senses, unmuted, engage in every experience. Moreover, there is no hesitance to be involved with the object perceived.[101]

Based on this articulated spirituality, the document highlights certain ritual emphases that mark African American Catholic worship:[102] (1) *space*: like the hush-harbors of the past, a worship space that "gives sway to the rich array of the auditory, tactile, visual, and olfactory senses," communicating both an African heritage and the struggle of Black Americans today; (2) *time*: an unfettered period of time that gives 'the Spirit breathing room" and time to "tell the ancient story"; (3) *action*: movements, gestures—"hands lifted in prayer, bowed heads, bended knee, jumping, dancing, shouting"—and bodily interaction that speak of the movements of the Spirit; (4) *the language of prayer and preaching*: vivid narrative, rhythmic intonations, poetry, witnessing, heartfelt calling on God—all signaling that "words are important" and that words become dialogic within the worshiping assembly; and (5) *sacred song*: the "soul" of African American liturgy, full of improvisation, creativity, spontaneity, and response.

---

98. *Plenty Good Room*, no. 49.
99. Leopold Sedar Senghor, as quoted in *Plenty Good Room*, no. 85.
100. *Plenty Good Room*, no. 86.
101. Rivers, *The Spirit in Worship*, 21.
102. Images in this section are taken from *Plenty Good Room*, nos. 89–99, 102.

In conclusion, the authors state that honing authentic African American Catholic worship is a process "of developing and continuing a tradition," and that this "laudatory and difficult task" needs to continue into the future, engaging the "pastoral sensitivity and academic excellence [of] liturgists, scholars, artists, musicians and pastors."[103]

Plenty Good Room was generally embraced by the African American Catholic community as a much needed affirmation of Black culture, spirituality, and religiosity. However, the limitations of the document could be readily identified. Two severe criticisms of the document were its frequent use of the terms "adaptation" and "accommodation" instead of "inculturation" and its implicit, if not explicit, endorsement of the rubrical prescriptions of the Roman rite as the normative model for Black Catholic worship.[104]

Adaptation or Inculturation

African American Catholics who wanted more self-determining participation within the Catholic Church pointed to the use of the term "adaptation" in *Plenty Good Room* as further proof of the persistent "White bias" of the American Catholic episcopacy. Criticism of this term was also being voiced about all Roman pastoral directives of that time by theologians and pastoral leaders throughout the larger Catholic community. By the end of the 1980s, the word "adaptation" was no longer understood as a "neutral" term.[105] It was now commonly equated with "cultural accommodation," a process that allows only superficial modifications in the Church's norms and practices and often involves the manipulation of culture to suit established pastoral conventions.[106] Thus, a significant number of African American Catholics thought the use of this term in *Plenty Good Room* demonstrated the disparity of pastoral vision that existed between the Black community and the U.S. episcopacy. They believed that the growing depth and breadth of the Black Catholic movement required a full embrace of liturgical "inculturation," an ongoing, reciprocal process between the faith and culture. This process radically imbues culture with the spirit and values of the gospel such that it is renewed, purified, and more consciously oriented to the ethical norms manifested by the life and teachings of Jesus Christ. At the same time, the faith tradition is embellished by the culture such that it is renewed, further developed, and expanded by the cultural gifts of a particular faith community.

Theologian Ary Roest Crollius gives further definition to the term inculturation by explaining it as a process that includes three distinct and necessary phases. Crollius calls the first phase *translation*. During this phase, local Church officials (presumably

---

103. *Plenty Good Room*, no. 123.
104. Ibid., nos. 110–122.
105. See Mark Francis, "Liturgical Adaptation," in *The New Dictionary of Sacramental Worship,* ed. Peter E. Fink (Collegeville, Minn.: Liturgical Press, 1990), 14.
106. See Anscar Chupungco, "A Definition of Liturgical Inculturation" *Ecclesia Orans* 5 (1985): 13; Aylward Shorter, *Toward a Theology of Inculturation* (Maryknoll, N.Y.: Orbis Press, 1988), 191–194.

of a different culture than the local community) learn to use the symbols and idiom of the people to promote the faith, and the people learn to articulate their beliefs, traditions, and values within the existing constructs of the faith tradition. Crollius names the second phase *assimilation*. In this phase, the faith tradition is no longer a stranger to the people, becuase there are indigenous pastoral leaders who exercise the principal role for nurturing the local community's faith. As this phase progresses, the local community's articulation and practice of the faith begins to demonstrate increasingly more cultural specificity, which inevitably develops into the third and last phase, *transformation*. At this point, the local faith community's experience of the religious tradition has become an integral part of their self-understanding, and the community's expression of the faith becomes synthesized with the primary symbol systems of its culture.[107] The critics of *Plenty Good Room* believed that the document promoted the second stage of inculturation for a community that had reached the third, or transformational stage. To support this claim, they readily referred to the Black Catholic bishop's 1984 pastoral letter, which states:

> The African-American Catholic community has now come of age. . . . The historical roots of Black America and those of Catholic America are intimately intertwined. Now is the time for us who are Black Americans and Black Catholics to reclaim our roots and to shoulder the responsibilities of being both Black and Catholic. The responsibility is both to our own people and to our own Church.[108]

While the first criticism of *Plenty Good Room* challenged its terminology, the second criticism challenged its goals. The document had been written as a companion to *In Spirit and Truth*.[109] Apropos to this, *Plenty Good Room* endorsed the Roman rite as the starting point, if not the normative model, for Black Catholic worship. This perception of the document fueled the ongoing discussion of an autonomous African American rite. In 1991, the National Black Catholic Clergy Caucus' African-American Catholic Rite Committee (AACRC) published a monograph entitled *Right Rites*.[110] The document was developed with a fourfold purpose: (1) it explained the nature and origin of Catholic canonical and liturgical rites; (2) it identified the Roman rite (also referred to as the Latin or Western rite) as one of the Catholic Church's twenty-three rites; (3) it outlined some of the pastoral concerns regarding the Black Catholic community; and (4) it offered a proposal for a study of an African American Catholic Rite that would be presented at the 1992 National Black Catholic Congress. This proposal read:

---

107. Ary Roest Crollius, "What Is So New about Inculturation?" *Gregorianum* 59 (1978): 733. See also Pope John Paul II, *Catechesis in Our Time* (Catechesi Tradendae) (Washington, D.C.: USCC Publishing Office, 1979), no. 53. John Paul II instructs catechists to both steep their learners in the faith tradition and to "call forth with original expressions of Christian life, celebration and thought."

108. Black Catholic Bishops of the United States, *Brothers and Sisters,* 17.

109. *Plenty Good Room,* v.

110. National Black Catholic Clergy Caucus, *Right Rites* (Opelousas, La.: African-American Catholic Rite Committee of the National Black Catholic Clergy Caucus, 1991).

> We urge the permanent body of the National Black Catholic Congress to initiate, coordi-
> nate, and support a comprehensive study to determine the desirability and feasibility of
> establishing an African American Catholic Rite.[111]

Right Rites urged the establishment of an African American Catholic Rite as an essential component of meaningfully addressing three urgent pastoral concerns: (1) the survival of Black Catholicism; (2) the cultural imperatives for effective Catholic evangelization; and (3) the need for Black Catholic leadership.[112] It maintained that the Catholic Church's failure to fully embrace the ethno-religious patrimony of Blacks was actually contributing to the demise of the African American Catholic community—forcing Black Catholics to look to other faith traditions and/or ideological foundations to address the pastoral issues that permeated their lives.[113] The NBCCC's monograph also charged that the Catholic Church's halfhearted evangelization efforts and Euro-dominant pastoral priorities were primary contributors to the Black community's growing "unchurched" population, as well as the growing number of Black Catholics who had begun to "supplement" their practice of Catholicism by frequenting other churches.[114] The monograph further maintained that the practice would inevitably continue until the Catholic Church actively pursued full inculturation.[115] Anything less would simply result in perpetuating the dependence of Blacks upon non-Black ecclesial leaders to "interpret the faith for them" and perpetuate the untenable conflicts that arise from Blacks always having to defend and justify their religious insights and sensibilities.

The Study of Opinions

The NBCCC distributed *Right Rites* to the National Black Catholic Congress Office's regional coordinators nationwide with the request that the publication be studied by the delegates to the 1992 National Black Catholic Congress. The proposal was unanimously supported by the congress delegates. In response, the National Black Catholic Congress Office conducted a random survey[116] of the African American com-

---

111. Leonard G. Scott, "Canonical Reflections on the Study Conducted by the National Black Catholic Congress Regarding the Establishment of an African American Rite," in *A Survey of Opinions of African American Catholics,* ed. National Black Catholic Congress (Baltimore: National Black Catholic Congress Office, 1995), 43.

112. National Black Catholic Clergy Caucus, *Right Rites,* 4.

113. Ibid. For a fuller discussion of the integral relationship between faith and culture see Robert J. Schreiter, *Constructing Local Theologies* (Maryknoll, N.Y.: Orbis Press, 1986), 149.

114. The Black bishops had already criticized the ways in which racism had "marred" U.S. evangelization efforts among Blacks. See Black Catholic Bishops of the United States, *Brothers and Sisters,* 3; Schreiter, *Local Theologies,* 144–158. Schreiter offers a detailed description of the nature of syncretism and dualism. For a description of some of the significant expressions of syncretism and dualism in the history of the Americas, see Raboteau, *Slave Religion,* 16–25, 285–288.

115. Schreiter, *Local Theologies,* 150.

116. National Black Catholic Clergy Caucus, *Right Rites.*

munity in April of 1994. A report of the survey findings was released in January of 1995 under the title, *A Study of Opinions of African American Catholics.*[117] Seventy-two percent of the respondents rejected the idea of an autonomous canonical rite, but a clear majority (64%) said they would welcome the possibility of developing liturgies that were more distinctively Black.[118] A more complete review of the survey data revealed that 79% of the respondents felt comfortable in their parish, while 51% felt the U.S. Church as a whole did care about them. Forty-five percent said their parish liturgies already included some form of Black religious expression. However, 50% also wanted more African American music, 59% wanted more African customs incorporated into their Sunday worship experience, 62% wanted more African customs incorporated into special religious events (e.g., baptisms and weddings), and 53% wanted a distinctive African liturgy developed for African American parishes. Another key indicator in the survey data revealed that almost 55% of the respondents believed that predominantly African American parishes should have African American pastors (24% disagreed).[119]

The National Black Catholic Office interpreted these findings by issuing a poignant challenge in the concluding statement of the survey report:

> The data shows [*sic*] very little support for, and a great deal of opposition to, the creation of a full canonical rite or for other opinions or proposals seen as separatist. . . . On the other hand, there is very strong and even widespread support for an increased African American focus in the church's life and worship, with only the older group offering a little less support. . . . *As a matter of ecclesial strategy, this suggests that the choice is between dealing with Increased African American Focus now or Separation later.*[120]

The report summary goes on to say that local rather than national initiatives to develop liturgies with more of an "African American focus" would be better supported due to the high level of confidence that the survey respondents expressed for their parish. The National Black Catholic Congress Office further proposed that ecclesial authoritative groups assist these efforts in the following manner:

> [B]oth authority groups and professional groups, might . . . envision their role as primarily removing roadblocks to local initiatives, sponsoring research and scholarship, providing opportunities for training of clergy, religious and lay leaders, and encouraging

---

117. National Black Catholic Congress, *A Survey of Opinions of African American Catholics* (Baltimore: National Black Catholic Congress, 1995). Forty-eight percent of the survey participants were deliberately selected from the national organizations of priests, men and women religious, deacons, and seminarians. Analysis of the survey data suggests that some of the laity who constituted the other 52% of respondents were not randomly selected but designated on the local level.

118. Ibid., 3.

119. Ibid., 7–16.

120. Ibid., 19–20. Italics ours.

parishes which are most successful at implementing a strategy of increased African America focus to share their stories with others.[121]

The survey report concluded with three reflection papers that explored the pastoral and theological implications suggested by the data. The first paper was written by Leonard G. Scott, an African American canon lawyer. Scott's review of the survey findings led him to conclude that the respondents showed tacit support for the creation of a liturgical rite, like the Roman Missal for the dioceses of Zaire, if not for an autonomous rite. He pointed out that both the Vatican II Constitution on the Liturgy and the Revised Code for Canon Law acknowledge that such rites may be needed so that people may "follow their own form of spiritual life consonant with the teaching of the Church."[122] Moreover, Scott concluded that the strong support for more of an "African American focus" in worship demonstrated that Black Catholics do not oppose separatism at the parish level.[123]

The second paper was written by Jamie Phelps, an African American theologian. She interpreted the survey data as an indication that African American Catholics of the 1990s have embraced two "major theological concepts prevalent within contemporary Catholic ecclesiology: the theology of inculturation and the theology of communion."[124] Phelps interpreted the survey findings as a sign of the African American community's conscious attempt to reclaim their identity as a people and celebrate it with the full rights, privileges, and obligations as other members of the Church. She called attention to the fact that inculturation of the Gospels, preaching, and liturgical celebration are essential to the "growth and nurturance of the life and well-being of African American Catholics."[125] She explained the rejection of an autonomous rite as a rejection of the "myth of racial inferiority" that once enforced American apartheid in society and the Church. Finally, Phelps proposed that research continue to be done so that the U.S. bishops, as well as other pastoral leaders, will be better equipped to design and implement effective pastoral strategies for/with the African American community.[126]

African American theologian Diana Hayes wrote the third and last paper. Her reading of the survey findings led her to deduce that the pastoral questions raised in the 1970s and 1980s were being answered in the 1990s. She highlighted the earlier questions in the following manner:

---

121. Ibid., 20.

122. Scott, "Canonical Reflections," 45.

123. Ibid., 50.

124. Jamie T. Phelps, "Ecclesiological Implications of 'The Study of Opinions of African American Catholics.'" in *A Survey of Opinions of African American Catholics,* ed. National Black Catholic Congress (Baltimore: National Black Catholic Congress, 1995), 53–54.

125. Ibid., 54.

126. Ibid., 52–53, 57.

How do we, as a people of African roots and American and other branches, come together to sing our songs of faith in a style and manner in which we are comfortable and at home? Must we adapt ourselves to the styles and forms of worship of our Euro-American brothers and sisters who, although they share our faith, do not share our historical experience of enslavement, oppression and continuing discrimination based solely on race, or can we be free to inculturate the Christian faith and its Catholic expression into our own culture and historical traditions showing that they are equally worthy and capable of nurturing and spreading the Gospel. Is there something distinctly "Black" about our expression of "church" which should not only be preserved but also fostered, taught, and passed down to oncoming generations while, at the same time, being shared as an enriching gift with all whom we come into contact![127]

According to Hayes, the survey data showed the awareness and resolve of a community that is decidedly Black and Catholic. African American Catholics are no longer asking for acceptance; they are asking for recognition and understanding. But, more than this, they are asking for reconciliation and healing in a Church marred by racism; and, if this is to happen, the larger Church and the Black community must interact as equals.[128] Hayes concluded by saying that African American liturgical innovations bear witness to their "coming of age" in ways that are "neither transient nor precipitate." Such innovations express the community's efforts for a fuller experience and expression of their faith tradition. In the last analysis, she says, "there is no turning back."[129]

With the survey completed, NBCCC's committee for an African American rite disbanded. Some African Americans questioned if the respondents would have given more support to an autonomous rite had they understood that it would be "in communion with Rome" while maintaining its own structures of governance. Others questioned how much the hurtful legacy of American apartheid, as well as the 1990s pastoral emphasis on "multiculturalism," had influenced the respondents' rejection of what seemed to be a separatist movement. Some questioned whether or not the respondents understood the significant role that their historic "separate church" experience had played in helping them to both name and develop their distinct ethno-religious identity.[130] Still others believed that the issue of an African American Catholic rite had been resolutely decided. However, the confluence of several developments within the larger Black community and the African American Catholic community during the early 1990s served to keep the discussion very much alive.

---

127. Diana L. Hayes, "My People Shall Never Again be Put to Shame," in *A Survey of Opinions of African American Catholics,* ed. National Black Catholic Congress (Baltimore: National Black Catholic Congress Office, 1995).

128. Ibid., 61–64.

129. Ibid., 66.

130. Ibid., 56. Phelps summarizes and responds to some of these questions in footnote 5 of her article.

Africentricity as a Means of Inculturation

One of the most important developments of the early 1990s was the growing popularity of "Africentricity"[131] as the galvanizing principle or philosophy within the African American community. African American Catholics were not unaffected by its insight or appeal. The African American scholar Molefi Asante had popularized the phrase "Afrocentricity" in 1980 to describe the activity of Black people around the world who were consciously reclaiming an African worldview, as well as the cosmic or metaphysical realm that determined what it meant for them to be human persons. By 1991 Asante had further developed the concept. He argued that this word, more than any other term (e.g., a Black interpretation, an African American perspective), denoted the deliberate effort of Black people to name themselves, value themselves, pursue their legitimate ambitions, and promote their insights from a self-conscious and self-accepting frame of reference. Moreover, Asante maintained that this philosophical stance did not seek to denigrate the inherent merits or worth of any other cultural heritage. It simply asserted that African culture represents an alternative vision to the worldview, epistemology, cosmology, normative assumptions, and axiological frames of reference that have dominated human discourse, human relationships, and human industry for the last five hundred years.[132]

While the ideational constructs of Africentricity are clearly evident in the theological and pastoral literature written by African American pastoral leaders throughout the 1970s and 1980s,[133] the word was formally introduced into Catholic pastoral literature in relationship to catechesis in 1995.[134] By that time the NCCB Subcommittee on Liturgy in the African American Community had been disbanded. In the absence of an episcopal committee sensitive to the liturgical needs and priorities of African Americans, the pastoral leadership of the African American community was left on its own to develop the community's liturgical life in more culturally relevant ways. As the decade progressed, pastoral leaders in various parts of the country created a rich constellation of liturgical innovations. The following list highlights only a sampling of the noteworthy examples. The National Black Catholic Congress Office published *Rise Up and Rebuild,* a ritually-based catechetical process that blends traditional Catholic prayer forms with characteristic elements of the African American prayer tradition in tradi-

---

131. The word "Afrocentricity" derives from the word "Afrology," the study of African concepts, issues, and behaviors. Molefi K. Asante, *Afrocentricity: The Theory of Social Change* (Buffalo: Amulefi, 1980), 67. Some African American scholars have reformulated the term "Afrocentricity" to "*afr*icentricity" noting that this word more explicitly depicts the disctinctiveness of "Africa" and encourages discussants to reflect on African culture, philosophy, values, etc., from an emic point of view.

132. Molefi K. Asante, *Afrocentrity* (Trenton, N.J.: African World Press, 1991), and Molefi K. Adsante, *The Afrocentric Idea* (Philadelphia: Temple University Press, 1987).

133. See Rivers, *Soulfull Worship;* National Office for Black Catholics, *This Far By Faith;* Posey, *Theology.*

134. Eva Marie Lumas, "The Nature and Goals of Africentric Catechesis," in *God Bless Them That Have Their Own,* ed. Therese Wilson Favors (Washington, D.C.: United States Catholic Conference of Bishops, 1995), 28–37.

tional African worship. A growing number of Black pastoral leaders began to incorporate elements of African naming ceremonies into their celebrations of the sacrament of Baptism and created rites of passage to enhance the preparation of Black youth for the sacrament of confirmation. Black leaders collaborated with the North American Forum on the Catechumenate to consider Africentric strategies for the Order of Christian Initiation for Adults. A nationally representative group of Black liturgical composers and musicians began work on a book of Black psalmnody. A cooperative of Black diocesan and parish pastoral leaders proposed ways to utilize African proverbs to explicate the Sunday gospel readings. A culturally distinct genre of liturgical prayers, blessings, and commissioning rites for parish ministers began to develop. Catholic liturgical celebrations of Black History Month became commonplace nationwide. The NBCCC designated November as Black Catholic History Month and encouraged the development of parish liturgical celebrations. The introductory rite of parish eucharistic celebrations sometimes included an invocation of the ancestors. The ethno-religious significance of the liturgical year began to be explored by Black pastoral leaders. The celebration of Kwanzaa began to influence the way that African American Catholics celebrated Christmastide. Liturgical dance became a more frequent occurrence in African American Catholic worship. Culturally specific ritual texts for the celebration of traditional Catholic devotions (i.e., Marian feasts) also began to emerge.[135]

Another development of significant importance in the 1990s was the creation of an African American Catholic liturgical journal named *Plenty Good Room*. The inaugural issue of *Plenty Good Room* appeared in June of 1993. The journal's editor, J-Glenn Murray, described the purpose of the publication as an aid for Catholic liturgical ministers who "strive for union of rite and culture" in the African American Catholic community.[136] The journal met with mixed reviews from the African American community. Its feature articles were generally lauded for the "continuing education" they provided for parish liturgical ministers, as well as the ongoing catechesis they provided to the larger parish community. However, the theological hermeneutic that undergirded the journal's "practical liturgical suggestions" was often criticized for being "too closely allied" with the rubrical boundaries, and therefore, the Eurocentric biases of the Roman rite. At the same time, this journal provided the only public forum in which the issues of African American liturgical inculturation could be regularly addressed.

Varietates legitimae

Within this pastoral and liturgical milieu, the Vatican's Congregation for Divine Worship and the Discipline of the Sacraments published a pastoral instruction entitled, *Inculturation and the Roman Liturgy (Varietates legitimae)* in 1994. The document

---

135. National Black Catholic Congress, *Rise Up and Rebuild: A National Black Catholic Congress VII Follow-Up Program.* (Baltimore: The National Black Catholic Congress Office, 1992). Most of the innovations cited are not yet published.

136. J-Glenn Murray, S.J., "Roots," *Plenty Good Room* (May/June 1993): 2.

states that its primary purposes are to define and/or further explain the forms for "adaptation of the liturgy to the temperament and conditions of different peoples, which were given in articles 37–40 of the constitution *Sacrosanctum Concilium*."[137] *Varietates legitimae* then affirms liturgical "inculturation" rather than "adaptation" as the normative approach for achieving its objectives. It calls for ongoing research and discernment regarding inculturation in response to each cultural community's "progressive maturity in faith" and highlights the ways in which this was done in the early Church as Christianity spread beyond the boundaries of Jewish religio-cultural communities.[138] The last three sections of *Varietates legitimae* outline the theological, pastoral, and canonical considerations that should guide all Roman Catholic liturgical inculturation. Included in these three sections are a series of foundational principles and guidelines that further explain the document's primary purposes: (1) to promote cultural adaptations already approved for use in the celebration of the Roman rite and (2) to preserve "the substantial unity of the Roman rite." Among the adaptations that were already approved, *Varietates legitimae* encouraged the liturgical use of a people's language, religious tradition, gestures and postures of prayer, and religious aesthetics (i.e., visual art, architecture, vestiture, the selection and arrangement of decorations, the location of the altar, and the place where the Scripture is proclaimed).[139]

With regard to preserving the unity of the Roman rite, *Varietates legitimae* articulates five explicit directives. First, it named the national conferences of bishops as the authorized agents to discern and oversee the manner in which any liturgical adaptations would be implemented and reserved ultimate authority for determining the merits of these endeavors for the Holy See.[140] Second, it identified essential criteria to be applied to the planning and implementation of liturgical inculturation, instructing the bishops to be mindful of the goal of inculturation, the substantial unity of the Roman rite, and the role of competent authority.[141] *Varietates legitimae* thus defined a twofold purpose for inculturation: it "responds to the needs of a particular culture and leads to adaptations which still remain part of the Roman rite."[142]

The third directive for liturgical inculturation focused on the need for prudence. It reminds the bishops that any and all adaptations being considered should "grow organically from forms already existing" within the Roman liturgical rites.[143] They are instructed to avoid adaptations that foster religious syncretism, cause a community to become inward looking or to use inculturation for political purposes, or promote the extreme cultural localization of liturgical celebrations.[144] Even in those instances when

---

137. Congregation for Divine Worship and the Discipline of the Sacraments, *Varietates Legitimae (Inculturation and the Roman Liturgy)* (Washington, D.C.: United States Catholic Conference, 1994), no. 3.

138. Ibid., nos. 9–20.

139. Ibid., nos. 38–52.

140. Ibid., nos. 21–27, 37, 62–69.

141. Ibid., no. 34.

142. Ibid., nos. 35–37.

143. Ibid., no. 46.

144. Ibid., nos. 46–51, 54.

the need for "radical adaptations" are considered, the document maintains that these changes will most often occur within the current context of the Roman rite, rather than necessitating a comprehensive transformation of the Roman rites.[145] The next directive, after naming some of the practical implications, reiterated the need for revisions of the liturgical books to insure that the Roman missal "remain a sign and instrument of unity" and only the approved texts, gestures, and order of service be used.[146] The fifth and final directive addresses those instances when "radical adaptations" to the rites are deemed necessary. Even in these instances, the Vatican document asserts that such changes will most often not "envisage" a transformation of the Church's liturgical rites."[147]

Within months of its publication, *Varietates legitimae* spawned a furor of debate among African American Catholics. Most agreed that the document simply affirmed the insights already articulated by *In Spirit and Truth* (1988) and *Plenty Good Room* (1990). However, many criticized the document for failing to acknowledge the plethora of liturgical insights and innovations that had developed in the thirty-plus years since Vatican II. For them, *Varietates legitimae* was further proof of the Catholic Church's ignorance, if not distrust, of culture and contradicted (or at least misrepresented) the pastoral insights of *Sacrosanctum Concilium,* as well as other counciliar and postcounciliar documents.

More than a Question of Starting Points

Critiquing the strengths and weaknesses of *Varietates legitimae* became the focus of a series of feature articles published in the liturgy journal *Plenty Good Room*. Then Marist Brother Cyprian Lamar Rowe wrote the first article. He ardently objected to the notion that "preserving the unity of the Roman rite" should be a guiding principle for inculturation because it placed predetermined limits on the process. Rowe maintained that compliance to *Varietates legitimae* would make African Americans little more than "cultural hostages," whose freedom to engage their ethno-religious identity with Catholicism at the most personal and compelling level is diminished, if not disallowed.[148] Simply put, Rowe charged that African Americans should not accede to the Vatican document's directives on inculturation without asking the question, "What gets lost?"

J-Glenn Murray, the journal's editor, responded to Rowe by conceding that *Varietates legitimae* did not offer the most insightful definition of inculturation,[149] but, since

---

145. Ibid., nos. 63, 70.

146. Ibid., nos. 54–62.

147. Ibid., no. 63.

148. Cyprian L. Rowe, "A Tale of War, A Tale of Woe," *Plenty Good Room* (September/October 1994): 11–13.

149. J-Glenn Murray, S.J., "Give and Take: A Response to War and Woe," *Plenty Good Room* (November/December 1994):7–8.

it was the only one "offered for the whole church's consideration," he chose to focus on the document's positive aspects. Murray also argued that the document's definition of inculturation was "serviceable" because it invited African Americans to create a place for themselves within the Roman rite.[150]

In a second article, Rowe criticized Murray's position on the grounds that it did not reflect the plethora of African American philosophical, theological, or pastoral insights.[151] He challenged Murray to attend to the deeper issues—to critique the insular cultural imperialism of *Varietates legitimae* that minimized the best of the Catholic Christian tradition, as well as the ethno-religious legacy of the African American community.[152] Rowe proposed that the gravity of the matter required an ongoing dialogue between the Holy See, the National Conference of Catholic Bishops, and a significant number of African American Catholics.[153] Murray responded to Rowe's second article by reviewing the many ways that the revised liturgical books already invited and embraced African American ethno-religiosity. He identified explicit parallels between the primary symbols of the Black struggle for liberation and the Christian hunger for salvation.[154] Murray then argued that part of the current emptiness that many African American Catholics experienced in Catholic worship is not the fault of the ritual, but rather the lack of cultural and liturgical insight on the part of those persons who prepare and participate in it.[155]

Murray then invited Richard McCarron, a Euro-American doctoral student and friend, into the dialogue. McCarron's article summarized the debate between Rowe and Murray and identified issues for ongoing reflection. He maintained that Rowe and Murray arrived at divergent conclusions regarding the merits of *Varietates legitimae* because their respective critiques had begun at different starting points.[156] Murray's position was rooted in the liturgical rubrics of the Roman rite; Rowe's was rooted in the distinctive ethno-religious patrimony of the African American community. McCarron further suggested that their conflicting understandings of liturgy revealed divergent ecclesiologies that should also be named and explored.[157] McCarron then challenged both Murray and Rowe through a series of questions. He questioned if Murray's defense of the Roman rite underestimated both the Eurocentric biases that undergird current liturgical norms and the spiritual quests of the African American Catholic community.[158] He

---

150. Ibid., 8, 10.
151. Cyprian L. Rowe, "A Tale of War, A Tale of Woe…Continued," *Plenty Good Room* (March/April 1995): 9–11.
152. Ibid., 11–13.
153. Ibid., 13.
154. J-Glenn Murray, S.J., "Doing the Rite Thing: A Further Response to 'War and Woe,'" *Plenty Good Room* (May/June 1996): 5–10.
155. Ibid., 11–12.
156. Richard E. McCarron, "Response to the Tales of War and Woe," *Plenty Good Room* (September/October 1996): 4–8.
157. Ibid., 8.
158. Ibid., 8.

also questioned if Rowe's insistence for an African American rite unduly discredited the ability of the Roman rite to facilitate the spiritual sojourn of African Americans and minimized the risks of insularity within the African American Catholic community.[159]

Before leaving the Roman Catholic Church to become a bishop of Imani Temple, Cyprian Rowe submitted a reply to McCarron. This time, Rowe not only criticized the Church's cultural imperialism, he also criticized the cultural insight of McCarron and Murray. Rowe reiterated that the critical flaw of *Varietates legitimae* was its attempt to anticipate the outcome of the inculturation process before it had begun.[160] Rowe expressed a concern that Murray's admitted ignorance of significant Black philosophers, theologians, scholars, and cultural theorists impeded his ability to interpret meaningfully *Varietates legitimae* for the African American community.[161] Specifically responding to the McCarron article, Rowe stated that his questions might have been even more helpful had they come from someone more knowledgeable of Black culture and religiosity.[162] The real problem, said Rowe, is one's starting point: if the Roman hierarchy, or anyone else, begins a dialogue about liturgical inculturation with the assumption that the liturgy and the discussants will not be changed, there is no real dialogue. There can never be authentic inculturation.[163] Both McCarron and Murray responded to Rowe's third article. McCarron restated that his article was meant to "raise issues and spark an ongoing dialogue."[164] Murray restated his support for the inculturation process that had begun and acknowledged that liturgical inculturation in the African American community could be greatly enhanced if it were better informed by the prophetic insights of more Black pastoral leaders.[165]

Murray then invited Black scholar Joseph A. Brown into the dialogue. Brown's article attempted to mediate what had become a highly emotional and personal debate. He affirmed Murray's credentials as a liturgist and as a Black Catholic leader. He proposed that Rowe's remarks did not represent the larger African American Catholic community so much as Rowe's own internal struggle while choosing to join the Imani Temple.[166] Brown never really answered Rowe's primary question, however: What get's lost—what does the Church in general, and African Americans in particular, have to give up in order to accommodate the traditional liturgical structures and expressions of the Roman rite?

---

159 Ibid., 8–9

160. Cyprian L. Rowe, "How Long, O Lord, How Long?" *Plenty Good Room* (July/August 1997): 4.

161. Ibid., 7–8.

162. Ibid., 8.

163. Ibid., 5–6, 8–10.

164. Richard E. McCarron, "A Response to Cyprian Lamar Rowe's 'How Long, O Lord, How Long?'" *Plenty Good Room* (July/August 1997): 12.

165. J-Glenn Murray, S.J., "A Response to Cyprian Lamar Rowe's 'How Long, O Lord, How Long?'" *Plenty Good Room* (July/August 1997): 12–13.

166. See Joseph A. Brown, "To Sit at the Welcome Table: A Meditation" *Plenty Good Room* (November/December, 1997).

Another article, volunteered by Scott Haldeman,[167] went more to the heart of the matter. He proposed that Murray and Rowe were arguing from a faulty essentialism. Haldeman affirmed that some African Americans are at home within the Roman rite, while others require more than the current norms can offer. Each one should have the freedom to satisfy their spiritual longings. He agreed that the question of what gets lost must be addressed. African Americans may choose to leave behind or suppress certain elements of their culture in order to fully embrace the rubrical norms of the Roman rite. But, he asked, are they choosing to leave these cultural elements behind, or are they being forced to do so?

No Turning Back

Ironically, the most emphatic criticism of *Varietates legitimae* was written by Reginald Whitt, who had argued against the creation of an African American rite just five years before. Whitt found *Varietates legitimae* to be noteworthy both for what it does say and for what it does not say.[168] He concluded that the strength of the document rests with its tacit support for the insights outlined by the National Conference of Catholic Bishops in 1987 and 1990, but he also presented a comprehensive critique of the document's weaknesses. Whitt's first criticism is directed toward the document's claim that *Sacrosanctum Concilium* did not envision inculturation efforts (then called liturgical adaptations) to "aim in the slightest at . . . transforming the Roman liturgical heritage."[169] Whitt maintains that the Vatican II document actually said nothing about maintaining the "substantial unity of the Roman rite" when discerning the need for a profound inculturation of the liturgy.[170] In fact, Whitt points out that article 40 of *Sacrosanctum Concilium* explicitly acknowledges that certain ethno-cultural and pastoral contexts might require the transformation of the Roman rite and/or the creation of new ritual structures.[171] Whitt then cites four relatively recent inculturation efforts that reflect definitive departures from the Roman ritual context: the restoration of the Ambrosian (1974) and the Hispano-Mozarabic (1988) liturgical rites, the creation of the Zairean liturgical rite (1988), and the Church's approval for at least five Roman Catholic congregations composed of former American Episcopalians to celebrate liturgy according to the rubrical norms of the Book of Divine Worship, which was originally developed for the Anglican Church.[172]

Whitt's second critical observation of *Varietates legitimae* deals with the fact that the document offers no guidance for liturgical inculturation within those ethno-cultural

---

167. Scott Haldeman, "Forging a New Self: A Response to War and Woe," *Plenty Good Room* (March/April 1998). Haldeman is the convenor of the study group on African American Worship Traditions of the North American Academy of Liturgy.

168. Whitt, *"Varietates Legitimae,"* 526.

169. Ibid.

170. Ibid., 527.

171. Ibid., 532.

172. Ibid., 514.

communities "whose religious culture is Christian but has not customarily been expressed within the Roman liturgy, for example, that of African Americans."[173] In this regard, Whitt warns that restricting the inculturation process of African American Catholics to the rubrical confines of the Roman rite may result in the manipulation of African American Christianity, which is essentially a non-Catholic Western faith tradition with its own "cultural and historical axis."[174] Apropos to this, Whitt suggests that the ongoing efforts of African American Catholics to develop their distinct ethnoreligious heritage may lead to the formulation of inculturated theologies that eventually require the creation of African American Catholic liturgical rites.[175]

Whitt's third criticism is that the document's selective references to *Sacrosanctum Concilium* as well as other counciliar and postcounciliar pastoral insights contributes little to the Roman Catholic Church's understanding of liturgy and to the integral relationship between liturgy and the broader cultural context that gives rise to a people's ethnoreligious patrimony.[176] He notes that the theological and pastoral cautions set forth in *Varietates legitimae* ignore the need to continually revise Roman liturgical books in light of the ongoing dynamics of cultural growth and change. He also points out that these endeavors may lead to "extensive adaptations" of the Roman ritual family, if not produce conclusive evidence of the need for an African American Catholic canonical rite.[177] Finally, Whitt encourages African American pastoral leaders to continue their inculturation efforts and the National Conference of Catholic Bishops to reexamine the pastoral impact of *In Spirit and Truth* and *Plenty Good Room*. His overall assessment of *Varietates legitimae* is that it "has breathed additional vigor into the issue of an 'African American Catholic rite.'"[178]

Whitt's 1997 article demonstrated a marked departure from his 1990 article, "Not Rite Now!" In the earlier article he had questioned whether or not African American Catholics had distinct spiritual and religious traditions. This later article revealed an understanding that even though the spiritual and religious traditions of Black Catholics had been suppressed within the Catholic Church, they were not destroyed.[179] African American Catholics had not simply "discovered" Blackness during the Civil Rights movement; they had begun to explore its legacy in more deliberate ways.[180] For Whitt and a sizable majority of African American Catholics, the time had come for the pastoral imperatives of Blackness and Catholicism to work together. Some African American Catholics may decide that full inculturation requires autonomy from the Church of Rome. Others may decide that inculturation can be achieved within the

173. Ibid., 530.
174. Ibid., 530–531.
175. Ibid., 531–532.
176. Ibid., 532.
177. Ibid., 532–534.
178. Ibid., 535–537.
179. See Guerin Montilus, "Culture and Faith: A Believing People," in *Tell It Like It Is: A Black Catholic Perspective on Christian Education*, ed. Eva Marie Lumas (Oakland: National Black Sisters' Conference, 1983), 35–44.; Black Catholic Bishops of the United States, *What We Have Seen and Heard*, 4.
180. Black Catholic Bishops of the United States, *What We Have Seen and Heard*, 8–10.

Roman ecclesial structure. In either case, African American Catholics will have the benefit of being intentionally, rather than habitually, Catholic.

Conclusion

> *"We will go, we shall go, we must go*
> *to see what the end can be."*[181]

As the third millennium of Christianity begins, it is clear that the emergence of a truly African American expression of Catholic liturgy has been, and continues to be, a complex, challenging, and dynamic endeavor. Over the last four decades, African American Catholics have engaged in a cultural renaissance that has led them to reclaim their distinct "ethno-religious patrimony" within the larger Church. They have also engaged in a spiritual renascence that has led to a forthright assertion that their embrace of Catholicism need not—indeed, must not—require the diminishment of their Blackness. Many issues, both liturgical and contextual, continue to be debated. New initiatives and leadership continue to emerge, and each gives witness to new expressions of joy and pain. Some are satisfied with the liturgical parameters of the Roman rite. Others are confident that the Church is open to the ongoing development of more culturally explicit worship within the African American community. Still others are convinced that Roman Catholic liturgical priorities and directives show more suspicion than support for the spiritual inheritance and quests of African Americans. Will this divergence of views encourage ongoing renewal within the Roman rite? Yes. Will it contribute to the Church's ongoing exploration of the relationship between faith and culture? Yes. Will it occasion the creation of African American liturgical rites? One has only to review the grassroots liturgical innovations of the last four decades to know that the answer to this question is also "Yes!" Only two questions are left unanswered: What role will the institutional structures of the Catholic Church choose to play in each of these endeavors? And what pastoral priorities will determine the role they choose?

If the Roman magisterium has definitively decided that "the time of experimentation is over," they can only succeed at forcing African Americans into antagonistic relationships with the Roman rite. If they are receptive to inculturation as an open-ended process, however, they can facilitate the spiritual maturity of the African American Catholic community in ways that will surely ennoble and enrich the whole Church. This understanding of inculturation will require the Church to actively encourage and support the theological inquiries, pastoral training opportunities, ritual experimentation, and ongoing dialogue advocated by Vatican II and most postconciliar liturgical directives. It will require an acknowledgement that Black Catholics must assume the leadership for directing these efforts. It will also require a commitment to

---

181. Based on the spiritual, "Done Made My Vow."

forthrightly address the unavoidable tensions and ambiguities of charting a course into an unknown future. Ultimately, it will require that everyone engaged in the enterprise presumes the unfailing providence of God, the pertinence of each person's contribution, and the inherent worth of an ethno-religious patrimony that is "authentically Black and truly Catholic."

The African American Catholic Hymnal and the African American Spiritual

M. Shawn Copeland

I

In the past four decades African American Catholics have done a good deal to animate and direct the inculturation of our faith and to transform and shape various aspects of our celebration of the Eucharistic Liturgy, our preparation for and reception of sacraments, our private and communal prayer, and, thus, our spirituality. The fine start on this endeavor owes much to the National Office for Black Catholics (NOBC), particularly, the untiring and imaginative leadership of Marianist Joseph Mary Davis, its first executive director, and Clarence Joseph Rivers, the doyen of Black Catholic liturgists. In the mid-1970s and early 1980s, through annual workshops, conferences, and the publication of its journal, *Freeing the Spirit,* as well as occasional monographs, the NOBC's program for Culture and Worship constructed a platform for the work of Black Catholic composers and liturgists such as Rivers, Rawn Harbour, Leon Roberts, Marjorie Gabriel-Burrow, Grayson Brown, Avon Gillespie, Eddie Bonnemere, and Ray East. These men and women molded and directed an African American renewal of Catholic worship, ritual, and forms of prayer. Thus, at least, to date, we may conclude that the primary impact of inculturation for African American Catholicism has been aesthetic, and the publication and widespread use of *Lead Me, Guide Me: The African American Catholic Hymnal*[1] is a singular example of this impact.

There were, perhaps, two proposals for a hymnal reflective of the spiritual, that is religious and cultural, sensibilities of Black Catholics. Avon Gillespie prepared a proposal for a hymnal in 1978. Three years later, Father James T. Menkhus, an associate pastor of St. Martin's in Baltimore, Maryland recognized the need for liturgical and devotional music reflective of his congregation.[2] In 1983, the National Black Catholic Clergy Caucus authorized the development of a hymnal and formed a committee

---

1. *Lead Me, Guide Me: The African American Catholic Hymnal* (Chicago: G.I.A. Publications,1987).
2. Jon Michael Spencer, *Black Hymnody: A Hymnological History of the African-American Church* (Knoxville: University of Tennessee Press, 1992), 193.

whose membership included professional musicians and liturgists as well as men and women who represented the commonality and plurality of the Black Catholic experience.[3]

In 1987, *Lead Me, Guide Me* was published by the Gregorian Institute of America, the major U.S. Catholic music publisher. The hymnal takes its name from a well-known hymn much beloved by Black Catholics, "Lead Me, Guide Me," composed in 1953 by Black gospel songwriter Doris Akers. It was dedicated to Father Clarence Rivers. Between its red, black, and green covers, *Lead Me, Guide Me* embraces the signature music of the twin heritages of Black Catholics: spirituals and Gregorian plain chant. Also included are gospel compositions, traditional and contemporary Catholic hymns in English and Latin, hymns composed by Dr. Watts and adapted to a Black idiom, and African American freedom songs.

As an aesthetic achievement of African American Catholic inculturation, *Lead Me, Guide Me* was "born of the needs and aspirations of Black Catholics for music that reflects both our African American heritage and our Catholic faith."[4] Still, beyond this crucial existential, there is a larger social and cultural setting to take into account. To appreciate the hymnal, we need to look to the confluence of three events: the Civil Rights movement of the 1960s, the Black Arts movement, and the Second Vatican Council. For Black Catholics, these events are nearly inseparable. The 1954 Supreme Court order to desegregate schools injected the Civil Rights movement with a new fervor and momentum that spilled over first into the Montgomery bus boycott of 1955, then into the sit-ins and freedom rides that took up the dangerous and daring struggle against legalized White racist regimes in the South. In the painful contest between King's Gandhian nonviolence and the students' angry cry for "Black Power," Black artists recognized the profound, even metaphysical, meaning of cultural self-determination. These artists grasped the need to reconnect aesthetics and ethics and refused to separate art from the whole of Black life, especially during that period of urban rebellion and social turbulence. Indeed, writer Larry Neal declared, "Black Art is the aesthetic and spiritual sister of the Black Power concept."[5]

Finally, in a number of ways, the Second Vatican Council enabled Black Catholics to enter deeply, fully, and authentically into the retrieval and appropriation of their cul-

3. Bishop James Patterson Lyke and Father William Norvel list the following, along with the organization each person represents, as members of the Black Catholic Hymnal Committee: Father Arthur Anderson, O.F.M., coordinating assistant; Edmund Broussard, Knights of Peter Claver and Ladies Auxiliary; Marjorie Gabriel-Burrow, National Association of Black Catholic Administrators; Bishop Wilton D. Gregory, the National Black Catholic Clergy Caucus; Avon Gillespie, who had developed a proposal for a hymnal in 1978; Rawn Harbor and Leon Roberts, the National Association of Black Catholic Musicians; Ronald Sharps, the National Office for Black Catholics; Brother Robert Smith, O.F.M. Cap., the National Black Seminarians Association; and Sister Laura Marie Kendricks, H.V.M., the National Black Sisters' Conference. "Preface," *Lead Me, Guide Me.*

4. Ibid.

5. Larry Neal, "The Black Arts Movement," in *Within the Circle: An Anthology of African American Literary Criticism from the Harlem Renaissance to the Present,* ed. Angelyn Mitchell (Durham and London: Duke University Press, 1994), 184.

ture and history, to protest and act on behalf of social justice, and to understand these activities as a liberating praxis. The council's impact on African American Catholics came through its repudiation of the Church's insularity and its identification with the world;[6] its insistence that the laity has a "special and indispensable role in the mission of the Church" and must not be deprived of "their rightful freedom to act on their own initiative";[7] its public affirmation of Catholic respect for individual conscience and religious freedom; and its serious interest in the contemporary problems of the day—the economic and political exploitation of peoples and countries of the so-called third world, the threat of nuclear war, disregard for the sanctity of human life, racism, and unbridled technological innovation.

Since the influence of the Second Vatican Council on Black Catholics has been a topic of frequent treatment, this article will sketch the Civil Rights movement and the Black Arts movement—social and cultural forces that made *Lead Me, Guide Me* possible, perhaps even necessary.[8] I will then turn to the inclusion of sixty-three African American spirituals in the hymnal, which is one more sign of Black Catholic self-affirmation of Black identity. A brief history of the spirituals may assist readers unfamiliar with their composition and dissemination. Finally, the article concludes with some sightings of the spirituals in Black Catholic life.

II

With the exception of the Supreme Court's 1896 decision of *Plessy* v. *Ferguson* perhaps, no judicial ruling on the civil rights of African Americans matches the significance of the Supreme Court's 1954 opinion in *Brown* v. *Board of Education of Topeka*. The *Plessy* decision admitted the inscription of the "separate but equal" doctrine onto the Constitution. By the end of the century, most of the Southern states had expanded their segregation regulations and passed Jim Crow laws, so that by 1908 streetcar segregation was common. Historian C. Vann Woodward observed that by the 1950s, law and/or custom had created and sanctioned "a racial ostracism that extended to churches and schools, to housing and jobs, to eating and drinking . . . all forms of public transportation, to sports and recreation, to hospitals, orphanages, prisons, and asylums, and ultimately to funeral homes, morgues, and cemeteries." This condition of segregation was held to be a "final settlement," a "permanent system" beyond alteration or change.[9] John Hope Franklin concluded his study of the history of legalized segregation in the United States in these words:

---

6. Vatican II, *Gaudium et Spes,* 7 December 1965.

7. Vatican II, *Apostolicam Actuositatem,* 18 November 1965, nos. 1, 24.

8. See Melva Wilson Costen, "Published Hymnals in the Afro-American Tradition," *The Hymn* 40, no.1 (January 1989): 17; also William Farley Smith, review of *Lead Me, Guide Me: The African American Catholic Hymnal, The Hymn* 40, no. 1 (January 1989): 13–14.

9. C. Vann Woodward, *The Strange Career of Jim Crow,* 3rd rev. ed. (New York: Oxford University Press, 1974), 7.

The law had created two worlds, so separate that communication between them was almost impossible. . . . The wall of segregation had become so formidable, so impenetrable, apparently, that the entire weight of the American tradition of equality and all the strength of the American constitutional system had to be brought to bear in order to make even the slightest crack in it.[10]

The Supreme Court's unanimous reversal of the *Plessy* decision in 1954 ignited the embers of the Civil Rights movement of the 1950s and 1960s and led to a response that the Court might *not* have intended. Standing on more than 350 years of protest, prayer, and hope, Black Americans "took the Supreme Court decision and made of it a heroic declaration of equality."[11] They understood the Court's decision as the fulfillment of an overdue promise and concluded that if segregation in education was wrong because of the invidious inequalities inherent in its very existence, then segregation itself was wrong and every manifestation of it ought to be abolished. Men, women, university students, and even children picked up the struggle for freedom with prayerful and bold courage.

Flush with the success of the Montgomery bus boycott, African Americans began campaigns of massive civil disobedience, refusing to tolerate any longer the abuses of White American racism. The freedom riders, young African American college students and their White counterparts, were notable in their commitment. Both Bernice Johnson Reagon and Robert Moses have written of how these young people set aside their studies to serve as sit-in leaders, voter registration organizers, office workers, and tutors in segregated rural and urban communities. In Mississippi, for example, local leaders like Amzie Moore, Reverend George W. Lee, C. C. Bryant, Jack Smith, and E. W. Steptoe instructed these young people in the critical reading of people and situations, supported them, housed them, fed them, nursed their wounds from beatings, and arranged their bail on arrest.[12] Already, Thurgood Marshall had made the NAACP (the National Association for the Advancement of Colored People) a household word. During these years, the nation became acquainted with grassroots Black organizations such as the Southern Christian Leadership Council (SCLC), the Congress on Racial Equality (CORE), and the Student Nonviolent Coordinating Committee (SNCC). However, these groups still maintained the gender line; the movement was clerical and male and could deal but haltingly with the leadership of plain-speaking, self-confident women like Ella Baker.

While Catholic participation in the Civil Rights movement would come later, Moses recalls "Father John LaBauve, a Catholic priest in Mound Bayou [Mississippi] whose

10. John Hope Franklin, "History of Racial Segregation in the United States," in *The Black Community in Modern America,* vol. 2 of *The Making of Black America,* ed. August Meier and Elliott Rudwick (New York: Atheneum, 1969), 12–13.

11. Albert B. Cleage, Jr., "The Black Messiah and the Black Revolution," in *Quest for a Black Theology,* ed. James J. Gardiner and J. Deotis Roberts, Sr. (Philadelphia: United Church Press, 1970), 2.

12. Bernice Johnson Reagon, "Let the Church Sing 'Freedom,'" *Black Music Research Journal* 4 (1987): 105; also Robert P. Moses, *Radical Equations: Math Literacy and Civil Rights* (Boston: Beacon Press, 2001), 23–57.

parish home Amzie [Moore] had used for voter registration workshops, [and who] had been transferred out of the Delta."[13] Catholics would be galvanized after the march on Washington in August 1963, the dreadful Sunday bombing of Birmingham's Sixteenth Street Baptist Church in September 1963 in which four young girls were killed, and the March 1965 march on Selma. Catholic participation in the interracial march on Selma was captured in a widely reprinted photograph featuring approximately a dozen priests in collars, including Black Catholic priest George Clements of the Archdiocese of Chicago, and four religious women in full habit, including Black Catholic Sister of St. Mary, Antona Ebo.

III

In the murky political environment spawned by the assassinations of President John F. Kennedy, Malcolm X, Dr. Martin Luther King, Jr., and Senator Robert Kennedy, the "aesthetic of integration" that King had charted in his "I Have a Dream" speech began to cede to an "aesthetic of separatism" promulgated by the Black Arts movement.[14] This was a defensive posture and protested the daily structural and systemic violence of anti-Black racism in America. The event considered to be the generative idea behind the Black Arts movement is the 1964 founding of the Black Arts Repertory/Theatre School in New York. This endeavor was lead by dramatist, critic, and poet LeRoi Jones (Amiri Baraka) along with several other Black artists. The theatre took its program of plays, concerts, and poetry readings to Harlem, Larry Neal wrote, with the intention of "shatter[ing] the illusions of the American body politic, and awaken[ing] black people to the meaning of their lives."[15] Although short-lived, the theatre inspired the formation of Black art groups in Los Angeles, Detroit, Chicago, Jersey City, New Orleans, Philadelphia, and Washington, D.C. The Black Arts movement was also the force behind the call for Black studies programs, which spread to many of the nation's college campuses.

Jones, Neal, Hoyt W. Fuller, Addison Gayle, Jr., Don L. Lee (Haki Madhubuti), and Ron Karenga were among the chief architects of the movement. Lee, in particular, acknowledged the talent and contributions of Black female artists like Gwendolyn Brooks and Mari Evans. For the most part, however, like the Civil Rights movement, the Black Arts movement stayed wide of the gender line.

Gayle's collection, *The Black Aesthetic,*[16] functioned as a kind of manifesto of the movement, although at least one earlier collection, *Anger, and Beyond,*[17] challenged

---

13. Moses, *Radical Equations,* 44.

14. Angelyn Mitchell, introduction to *Within the Circle: An Anthology of African American Literary Criticism from the Harlem Renaissance to the Present,* ed. Angelyn Mitchell (Durham and London: Duke University Press, 1994), 9–10.

15. Neal, "The Black Arts Movement," 188.

16. Addison Gayle, Jr., *The Black Aesthetic* (New York: Doubleday, 1971).

17. Herbert Hill, ed., *Anger, and Beyond* (New York: Harper and Row, 1966).

Black writers to place their creative imagination at the service of the freedom and dignity of Black people. In his introduction to *Anger, and Beyond,* Herbert Hill declared:

> In the future, Negro authors will not be writing as some did in the past, to please or titillate white audiences; they will not be telling of quaint and amusing colored folks or of exotic sensual Negroes who exist only in the fantasies of white people living in a society tragically obsessed by race and color.[18]

Black writers, Hoyt Fuller argued, did not reject universals, but rather the "assumption that style and language and concerns of [whites] establish the appropriate limits and frame of reference for black [art] and people."[19]

The most enduring slogan of the Black Arts movement was "Black is Beautiful," and it was shouted with relish at every opportunity. James Brown's recording of "Say It Loud, I'm Black and I'm Proud" was a popular standard. This aesthetic affirmation signified the release of women and men from centuries of oppression and self-hatred and the repudiation of any type of imitation of whites as a standard for life and art. To accept that "Black is Beautiful," Gayle asserted, was the first step in recovering from the "cultural strangulation" of Black life and Black art under the dominant White aesthetic and constructing a new and Black aesthetic.[20] Finally, one of the chief aims of the Black Arts movement was to reconnect aesthetics and ethics. To effect this, Neal argued that the Black artist must take the perspective of the oppressed: "In a context of world upheaval, ethics and aesthetics must interact positively and be consistent with the demands for a more spiritual world."[21]

The Black Arts movement called for a disengagement with the aesthetic values of White America. Black dramatists, critics, poets, and novelists sought a distinct standard for themselves, their art, and their people. They found its characteristic features of authentic self-regard, disciplined improvisation, polyrhythms, asymmetry, intensity, irony, and sarcasm in music—in particular, jazz. A generation later, Cornel West would make the same assessment and measure his own *oeuvre* by that of John Coltrane.

It is not possible to say with complete confidence just which Black Catholics were reading these critics, dramatists, and poets; if the regular gatherings of Black religious and clergy in Detroit and Chicago in the late 1960s and early 1970s can be taken as some measure, there were quite a few. Black Catholics have never been complete strangers to their culture, but the early contributions of Father Clarence Rivers, Father (now Bishop) Moses Anderson, S.S.E., Cyprian Rowe, and Sister Francesca Thompson, O.S.F., and then later those of Sister Thea Bowman, F.S.P.A., Father Joseph A. Brown, S.J., and Sister Eva Regina Martin, S.S.F., would reveal deep, critical immer-

18. Ibid., xxii.

19. Hoyt W. Fuller, "Towards a Black Aesthetic," in *Within the Circle: An Anthology of African American Literary Criticism from the Harlem Renaissance to the Present,* ed., Angelyn Mitchell (Durham and London: Duke University Press, 1994), 203.

20. Addison Gayle, Jr., "Cultural Strangulation: Black Literature and the White Aesthetic," in *Within the Circle: An Anthology of African American Literary Criticism from the Harlem Renaissance to the Present,* ed. Angelyn Mitchell (Durham and London: Duke University Press, 1994), 212.

21. Neal, "The Black Arts Movement," 186.

sion and appropriation of the wealth of African and African American literary, musical, historical, and material culture.

IV

I cannot say precisely when I first heard a spiritual, but I will forever associate the experience with my grandmother's singing on Sunday mornings after Mass. My maternal grandmother, Mattie L. Hunt Billingslea, was the last of eight children born to James and Mary (nee Hunt) Hunt in Macon, Georgia, early in the last century. Not long after the First World War, her widowed mother and enterprising brothers moved their family to Detroit, Michigan. Although the family attended Quinn Chapel African Methodist Episcopal Church, sometime in the 1940s my grandmother became a Catholic. She was baptized in Sacred Heart Church, one of the three or four churches in the archdiocese that seems to have been reserved for Black Catholics. In my childhood we were members of Holy Ghost parish, whose small, segregated, and demanding elementary school I attended. Each Sunday, one of the Spiritans (we knew them as Holy Ghost Fathers) celebrated the children's Mass. It was no different than the earlier or later Masses, but the priest would step away from the lectern (pulpit would be much too pretentious to describe the outfitting of our basement mission church), stand close to the communion rail, and explain the gospel directly and simply, but not, I think, condescendingly. Although my grandmother already would have heard Mass, when I returned home I was expected to summarize the gospel and give something of the homily. What I remember so well is that very often when I opened the front door, her rich alto would be raised in a spiritual. Much later, when I heard other Black Catholics tell similar stories, I recognized such singing of spirituals as a conserving, healing, even compensatory religious and psychic practice.

The spiritual, created by enslaved women and men, is rivaled, perhaps, only by jazz as the most widely known of all African American musical genres.[22] While it is difficult to date with any precision the origin of these songs, historians Miles Mark Fisher and Dena J. Epstein argue that the spirituals can be traced to the early eighteenth century.[23] Certainly the brutal social conditions (legalized and perpetual servitude, racial stigma, physical abuse, and alienation) of their composition were already in place by that time.

---

22. John Lovell, Jr., *Black Song: The Forge and the Flame—The Story of How the Afro-American Spiritual Was Hammered Out* (1972; reprint, New York: Paragon, 1986), 400. This work treats more than 375 years of the history of the African American spiritual; it is steeped in the flavoring of six thousand songs and refers to or cites directly more than five hundred of them. Other scholarly studies of the spirituals include Howard Thurman, *Deep River and the Negro Spiritual Speaks of Life and Death* (Indiana: Friends United Press, 1975); James H. Cone, *The Spirituals and the Blues: An Interpretation* (Westport, Conn.: Greenwood Press, 1972), LeRoi Jones, *Blues People: The Negro Experience in White America and the Music That Developed from It* (New York: William Morrow, 1963); Jon Michael Spencer, *Protest and Praise: Sacred Music of Black Religion* (Minneapolis: Fortress Press, 1990).

23. Miles Mark Fisher, *Negro Slave Songs in the United States* (New York: Citadel Press, 1953); Dena J. Epstein, *Sinful Tunes and Spirituals: Black Folk Music to the Civil War* (1977; reprint, Urbana and Chicago: University of Illinois Press, 1981).

Reports about the distinctive singing and dancing of the enslaved people drifted northward only gradually through travelers' chronicles, newspaper and journal articles, diaries of missionaries and teachers, novels, and the speeches and narratives of fugitive slaves.[24] Anglo-American and European visitors to the antebellum South were struck by the singing and dancing of the enslaved peoples. Many dismissed the songs as "uncouth barbarism, [while] others were stirred by the vigor of the dancing and the weird sadness of the songs."[25] To be sure, Southerners had mentioned the singing and dancing of the enslaved peoples, but usually as evidence of the Africans' contentment with their condition. The White men and women of the South deemed it "bad policy to give slaves credit for any type of cultural achievement."[26]

Because of their biblical content, the spirituals are associated with the Christianity of the enslaved Africans, but the Middle Passage did not completely eradicate religious practices, aspects and apprehension of material culture, social and religio-cultural beliefs, and cognitive orientations or ways of thinking about reality, life, and relationships.[27] The traditional religions of Africa formed the first stratum of the religio-cultural world of the enslaved peoples. These religions were, and remain, highly particular rather than universal. Yet, beneath the diversity of so many peoples, common modes of perception, common values, and common patterns of ritual can be discerned. For Africans, religion permeated every domain of human life. The whole of the universe radiated and mediated forces of the sacred—the supreme Deity, the divinities, and the spirits. There was no "formal distinction between the sacred and the secular, between the religious and non-religious, between the spiritual and the material areas of life."[28] Thus, religion occupied the whole person and the whole of a person's living. The most ordinary and the most extraordinary tasks and activities of daily life, human relationships, social interactions, and natural phenomena were suffused with religious understandings and meanings.

In addition to a supreme Deity and various lesser divinities or gods, Africans had to take into account their ancestors. These honored dead, both those who died long ago and the deceased of more recent memory, remained, even in death, most intimately connected to the living. Because they are believed capable of intervening in daily affairs—bestowing blessing or meting out punishment—the ancestors had to be ritually venerated according to custom.[29]

---

24. Epstein, *Sinful Tunes,* 161–183, 215–237, 241–302.

25. Sterling Brown, "The Spirituals," in *The Book of Negro Folklore,* ed. Langston Hughes and Arna Bontemps (New York: Dodd, Mead and Company, 1958), 279.

26. Lovell, *Black Song,* 400.

27. Joseph E. Holloway, ed., *Africanisms in American Culture* (Bloomington and Indianapolis: Indiana University Press, 1990), 2–13; Albert Raboteau, *Slave Religion: The 'Invisible Institution' in the Antebellum South* (Oxford: Oxford University Press, 1975), 5–7; Martha Washington Creel, *"A Peculiar People": Slave Religion and Community-Culture among the Gullahs* (New York: New York University Press, 1988), 29–50.

28. John Mbiti, *African Religions and Philosophies* (Garden City, N.Y.: Doubleday/Anchor, 1970), 2.

29. E. Bolaji Idowu, *African Traditional Religion: A Definition* (Maryknoll, N.Y.: Orbis Books, 1975), 184.

In traditional African religions, there were no sacred scriptures to be proclaimed and exegeted, no creeds to be studied and memorized, no dogmas to claim assent and observance. Religion "is written not on paper but in people's hearts, minds, oral history, rituals and religious personages like priests, rainmakers, officiating elders and even kings."[30] Ritual and ceremonial practices were central to marking rites of passage or initiation, funerals, births, and coronations or installation of chiefs. Singing, dancing, drumming, and creating and reciting poetry were essential interrelated components of these rituals.

Still, the Christianization of the enslaved Africans remains a disputed issue. Scholars cannot isolate each discrete moment from authentic efforts to evangelize and catechize enslaved Africans to the appearance of Black Christian churches. What we know unequivocally is this: Anglo-American Christianity, as the preaching of salvation in Jesus of Nazareth, had a decisive impact on the enslaved peoples. In turn, these men and women shaped and "fitted" Judeo-Christian practices, rituals, symbols, myths, and values to their own particular social experiences, religio-cultural expectations, and personal needs; these traditions helped the slave community to form an image of itself.[31] At the same time, because so very much of the intimate life of the enslaved peoples was hidden from the master class—indeed, from nearly all Whites—it is not possible to pronounce with certainty the burial of the gods of Africa and the complete disappearance of the traditional religions that honored them. When enslaved Africans moaned

> I've been 'buked an' I've been scorned,
> Dere is trouble all over dis worl',
> Ain' gwine lay my 'ligion down, Ain' gwine lay my 'ligion down,

we can never be completely sure *which* religion they were refusing to surrender.

Most historians and cultural anthropologists would agree that on plantations, religion was the sphere in which the enslaved Africans generally were able to exercise some measure of autonomy and freedom in intelligence, action, and creativity; still, they did so often at the risk of grave punishment. The attitudes and practices of slave holders regarding the religious activities of slaves have been well documented. On some plantations the enslaved peoples were permitted to hold independent, and sometimes, unsupervised worship services; on other plantations they attended White churches, sitting or standing in designated areas. On still other plantations the enslaved people were punished for praying and singing. Yet, from snatches of stories from the Scriptures, sermons, and their own critical reflections, the enslaved peoples fashioned "an inner world, a scale of values and fixed points of vantage from which to judge the world around them and themselves."[32]

---

30. Mbiti, *African Religions and Philosophies,* 5
31. Raboteau, *Slave Religion,* 213.
32. C. Johnson and A. P. Watson, eds., *God Struck Me Dead* (Philadelphia and New York: Pilgrim Press, 1969), vii.

Poet and literary critic James Weldon Johnson held that many spirituals were the work of highly gifted individuals whom he called in a celebrated poem "black and unknown bards."[33] Novelist and folklorist Zora Neale Hurston maintained that the spirituals were "Negro religious songs, sung by a group, and a group bent on expression of feelings and not on sound effects."[34] When asked about their method of composing their religious songs, enslaved men and women often replied: "De Lord jes' put hit en our mouf. We is ignorant, and de Lord puts ebry word we says en our mouf."[35] A former enslaved woman from Kentucky insisted that the spirituals were formed from the material of traditional African tunes and familiar songs:

> Us ole head use ter make 'em on de spurn of de moment, after we wressle wid de Spirit and come thoo. But the tunes was brung from Africa by our grandaddies. Dey was jis 'miliar song. . . . Dey calls 'em spirituals, case de Holy Spirit done revealed 'em to 'em. Some say Moss Jesus taught 'em, and I's seed 'em start in meetin'. We'd all be at the 'prayer house' de Lord's Day and de white preacher he'd splain de word and read whar Ezekiel done say: Dry bones gwine ter lib again. And, honey, de Lord would come a-shining thoo dem pages and revive dis ole [woman's] heart, and I'd jump up dar and den and holler and shout and sing and pat, and dey would all cotch de words . . . dey's all take it up and keep at it, and keep a-addin to it and den it would be a spiritual.[36]

Widespread "discovery" of the spiritual coincides with the Civil War and the inevitable close and direct contact between northern White soldiers and enslaved people, including Black soldiers. The most well-known record of such encounters is provided by Thomas Wentworth Higginson. A New Englander, Unitarian clergyman, and abolitionist, Higginson took command in November 1862 of the First South Carolina Volunteers, a regiment consisting largely of freed slaves from the Sea Islands.[37] In an article that he prepared for the *Atlantic Monthly,* Higginson commented on the men's singing of religious songs and offered an extended description of a shout.[38]

The first attempt at a serious and systematic collection of songs composed by the enslaved peoples appeared in 1867. *Slave Songs of the United States* was compiled by three Northerners, William Francis Allen, Charles Pickard Ware, and Lucy McKim Garrison, who was the inspiration behind the effort.[39] In June of 1862, McKim ac-

---

33. James Weldon Johnson and J. Rosamond Johnson, *The Books of American Negro Spirituals,* 2 vols. (1925; 1926; 1969; reprint, New York: Da Capo Press, 1989), 11–12.

34. Zora Neale Hurston, *The Sanctified Church* (Berkeley: Turtle Island, 1983), 80.

35. M. V. Bales, "Some Negro Folk Songs of Texas," in *Follow De Drinkin' Gou'd,* ed. James Dobie (Austin: Texas Folklore Society, 1928), 85.

36. Raboteau, *Slave Religion,* 244–45.

37. Leon F. Litwack, *Been in the Storm So Long: The Aftermath of Slavery* (New York: Knopf, 1979; New York: Random House, 1980), 68–69.

38. Thomas Wentworth Higginson, "Leaves from an Officer's Journal," parts 1 and 2, *Atlantic Monthly* 14 (November 1864): 521–29; (December 1864): 740–48.

39. William Francis Allen, Charles Pickard Ware, and Lucy McKim Garrison, comps., *Slave Songs of the United States* (1867; reprint, Bedford, Mass.: Applewood Books, 1995).

companied her father James Miller McKim to the Sea Islands of South Carolina. James McKim was an agent of the Philadelphia-based Port Royal Relief Committee, one of several voluntary groups organized by Northern anti-slavery people to recruit teachers, missionaries, and administrators to work with the emancipated slaves and to raise money for their salaries and supplies of food, clothing, and equipment. Lucy accompanied her father on a three-week tour of inspection and acted as his secretary. Her "perceptive enthusiasm" for the music prompted her to transcribe what she heard.[40] From Philadelphia daughter and father corresponded with John Dwight, editor of *Dwight's Journal of Music,* who published a small collection of the songs along with remarks by James McKim.[41] Lucy McKim's initial efforts to disseminate the religious and work songs of the enslaved people met with little public interest, but her collaboration with Allen and his cousin Ware, each of whom had begun to collect slave songs, bore fruit in a "book of permanent historical value."[42] However, the most definitive role in introducing the songs of the enslaved peoples to the world outside their tightly drawn circle of culture belongs to Fisk University.

In the decade following the Civil War, a number of church groups dedicated themselves to the education of the newly freed people. Fisk University, founded by the American Missionary Association of the Congregational Church, opened its doors in January 1866 to all students regardless of race. Although many of its teachers worked for little or nothing, by 1870 Fisk was on the verge of bankruptcy. George L. White, a teacher of music, suggested a concert tour to raise funds and to publicize the school. Despite the opposition of the school's trustees, White formed a singing group of nine Fisk students, all but one former slaves. From 1871 to 1875, the group, which became known as the Jubilee Singers, gave concerts in northern cities as well as England, Scotland, and Germany, singing the spirituals they had learned from their enslaved parents.[43] The perseverance and simple goodness of these young men and women in the face of rejection, discrimination, mockery, and ridicule at home and abroad made them heroic; Fisk University's Jubilee Hall made them legendary.

V

In their original settings, the creation and singing of the spirituals were marked by flexibility, spontaneity, and improvisation. The pattern of call-response allowed for the rhythmic weaving or manipulation of time, text, and pitch, while the response or repetitive chorus provided a recognizable and stable foundation for the extemporized lines

---

40. Epstein, *Sinful Tunes,* 256, 288.

41. Ibid., 288.

42. Ibid., 303.

43. Lovell, *Black Song,* 402–422; see also Andrew Ward, *Dark Midnight When I Rise: The Story of the Jubilee Singers Who Introduced the World to the Music of Black America* (New York: Farrar, Straus, and Giroux, 2000).

of the soloist or leader.[44] Hurston insisted that the spirituals are best appreciated when we imagine them, not concertized with dissonances "ironed out," but moaned in jagged irregular harmony, falsetto breaking in and keys changing with emotion.[45] W. E. B. DuBois called the spirituals "sorrow songs"[46] and, as such, perhaps, they are best understood when we imagine them in intimate mystical or ritual settings—cabins of rough wooden planks, "woods, gullies, ravines, and thickets" (aptly called brush arbors or hush arbors).[47]

The spirituals are inextricably bound to African American adaptations of religious rituals that invariably included hand clapping or the stomping of feet, which would have compensated on many plantations for the outlawed drum. However, the spiritual is linked most intimately to the staid shuffling of the *ring-shout*. A distinct form of worship, the ring-shout is basically a dancing-singing phenomenon in which the song is danced with the whole body—hands, feet, shoulders, hips. When the spiritual was sounded, the ring-shout would begin. The dancers formed a circle and moved counterclockwise in a ring, first by walking slowly, and then by shuffling—the foot just slightly lifted from the floor. Sometimes the people danced silently; most often they sang the chorus of the spiritual as they shuffled. At other times the entire song itself was sung by the dancers. Frequently, a group of the best singers and tired shouters stood at the side of the room to "base" the others, singing the body or stanzas of the song and clapping their hands. The dancing and singing would increase in intensity and energy and sometimes went on for hours.[48]

In creating the spirituals, the singers drew heavily and selectively on material "picked up . . . rather than read from" the Old and New Testaments. Nearly all slaveholders denied the teaching of even rudimentary reading and writing to enslaved Africans, and several southern states made this law. Slaves caught writing could be penalized by having a forefinger cut from the right hand.[49]

Biblical places most conspicuous in the spirituals include the Jordan River, Egypt, the Red Sea, Canaan, and Galilee. The people of the Old Testament who appear with some frequency in the songs include Abraham, Jacob, Moses and the Israelites, Pharaoh, Joshua, David, Ezekiel, Jonah, Daniel, and the three Hebrew Children—Shadrach, Meshach, and Abednego. Jesus is highly featured, particularly his birth, crucifixion, death, and resurrection; also prominent are Mary, Jesus's mother; John the

---

44. Portia K. Maultsby, "Africanisms in African-American Music," in *Africanisms in American Culture*, ed. Joseph E. Holloway (Bloomington and Indianapolis: Indiana University Press, 1990), 193.

45. Hurston, *Sanctified Church*, 80.

46. W. E. B. DuBois, *The Souls of Black Folk* (1903; New York: Vintage Books/Library of America, 1990), 180.

47. Raboteau, *Slave Religion*, 215.

48. Ibid., 70–71.

49. Lovell, *Black Song*, 257; see also Janet Duitsman Cornelius, *When I Can Read My Title Clear: Literacy, Slavery, and Religion in the Antebellum South* (Columbia, S.C.: University of South Carolina Press, 1991).

Baptist; the apostles John, Peter, Thomas, and Paul; Nicodemus; Mary and Martha of Bethany; Mary Magdalene; and Lazarus.[50]

The vocabulary or rhetoric of the spirituals is intensely poetic and expressive, decorative and poignant. It is characterized by vivid simile, creative and effective juxtaposition of images, and metaphor. Grounded in the experience of oppression, this highly charged symbolic language is most fundamentally a rhetoric of survival and resistance. The spirituals are unambiguously clear that "none but the righteous shall see God" and that the wicked shall be punished, but never are these songs tainted by any scent of hatred or references to vengeance. The Christianity of the spirituals is a religion of reconciling redemptive love. These songs dug the foundation for the successive waves of the struggle for freedom and civil rights and watered the stream of cultural retrieval and reappropriation. The spirituals are songs sung in hope of liberation in the context of a wilderness, but one in which God is at work, daily, hourly, to bring justice to completion.

VI

The publication of *Lead Me, Guide Me* was welcomed by reviewers. Black Protestant hymnologists Melva Costen and Jon Spencer were quick to recognize the role of the Civil Rights movement and the Black cultural revolution in prodding Black Catholics to explore and embrace their identity.[51] Wendelin Watson commented on the fusion of the Black and Catholic aesthetic liturgical traditions:

> The very appearance of *Lead Me, Guide Me* is striking and makes a distinct statement regarding the strong African-American heritage of Black Catholics. It has a hardbound laminated cover in the colors of the Black American liberation flag—red, black, and green—which symbolize the Black heritage and solidarity with African peoples. The flags of many African countries are made up of these colors which symbolize the shed blood, the race/color, and the land of its peoples. The title, *Lead Me, Guide Me,* appears at the bottom of the front cover in bright green letters against a Black and red design characteristic of African kinte [sic] cloths.[52]

Watson also noticed the use of Catholic symbols on the cover: on the front, the large capital letter *P*, evoking the Greek symbol *chi-ro,* used among early Christian communities to represent Christ, and, on the back, the stylized letter *M,* a Marian tribute.[53]

---

50. Lovell, *Black Song,* 258, 260–61.

51. Costen, "Published Hymnals in the Afro-American Tradition," 17; Spencer, *Black Hymnody,* 187.

52. Wendelin J. Watson, review of *Lead Me, Guide Me: The African American Catholic Hymnal, The Journal of Black Sacred Music* 3, no. 1 (Spring 1989): 69.

53. Ibid.

Cover design of Lead Me, Guide Me.

One of the earliest attempts to incorporate spirituals into European American Christian liturgical traditions may well have occurred in 1934 through the work of an Episcopal priest at the "Negro mission" of St. Simon of Cyrene, near Cincinnati, Ohio. This successful effort was documented by Sister Esther Mary, N.C.T. in her article, "Spirituals in the Church."[54] In a lecture at the first meeting of the Black Catholic Theological Symposium, Rivers recalled a similar experiment, one not nearly so successful. Rivers commented on the attempt by a religious sister in Oklahoma to bring together Black culture and Catholic worship:

> [Sister] attempted to cover the language of the Latin Mass with unadapted melodies from Negro spirituals. I remember the Kyrie was sung to the exact tune of "Nobody Knows the

---

54. Sister Esther Mary, N.C.T., "Spirituals in the Church," *The Southern Workman* 63 (1934): 308–314.

Trouble I See." The melody was an ill fitting garment for the words, however noble the idea behind the effort. . . . But I do remember someone saying around that time that Sister might have been more successful had she tried to adapt the basic style and the various elements of Black music to the needs of our liturgical texts without forcing, as it were, a shotgun wedding of existing melodies with incompatible texts.[55]

It is likely that Rivers would have found Sister Mary's argument for the use of spirituals in liturgical settings quite compatible with his own thinking. "The value of using spirituals in the service of a Church ministering to Colored people," she asserted, "seems to me to be threefold—the spirituals are a natural means of religious expression of the Negro people, they possess a beauty not dependent upon training and voice, [and] they offer a wealth of truly fine religious meanings."[56] Rivers recognized the contribution that the spirituals might make to what he called "effective worship"—that is, an instance of "humanly felt, perceived spiritual renewal/metanoia/uplift/healing." He grasped their essential simplicity, their "magnitude."[57]

VII

The Institute for Black Catholic Studies (IBCS) continues as a foremost site of Black Catholic intellectual and cultural research and liturgical experimentation. The spirituals hold a treasured and commanding place in the institute. Not only are the spirituals sung frequently at daily morning prayer and daily Eucharist, they figure prominently in the annual ceremony of the Commemoration of Ancestors. Moreover, the spirituals are the topic of a course taught regularly at the institute, and along with the slave narratives (oral histories generated from interviews with former slaves and their descendants through the Federal Writers Project in the late 1930s), they constitute primary source material for courses on Black spirituality, Black approaches to Scripture, and African American religious experience. In July 1993, New York-based folk artist Reginald Wilson, director of Reginald Wilson's Fist and Heel Performance Group, was invited to conduct a special seminar at the institute on the ring-shout, the holy dance that often accompanied the singing of spirituals during the period of enslavement. After a lecture and breathing and body exercises, Wilson lead a group of IBCS participants in a most prayerful engagement with this centuries-old holy dance.

Singing the spirituals as my grandmother did, as we do at the institute, and as so many Black Catholics have done and continue to do is a way of reaching inward to what liturgist and composer Grayson Brown identified as that *something* that is already

---

55. Rivers, "Thank God We Ain't What We Was," 68.
56. Mary, "Spirituals in the Church," 309–310.
57. Clarence Joseph Rivers, *The Spirit in Worship* (Cincinnati: Stimuli, 1978), 198, 199.

within us but to which we may need a reintroduction.[58] Another way to say this is that we are trying to come home to ourselves. That homecoming may be the recognition of a cultural or cognitive orientation; it may be an admission of a hunger for polyrhythm, asymmetry, improvisation, and the drum; or it may be surrender to a yearning for release, for vision. No matter: the spirituals and *Lead Me, Guide Me* are important vehicles for African American Catholics in our journey.

---

58. Grayson Warren Brown, "Music in the Black Tradition," in *This Far By Faith: American Black Worship and Its African Roots* (Washington, D.C.: NOBC and the Liturgical Conference, 1977), 93.

This Is My Story, This Is My Song: The Historiography of Vatican II, Black Catholic Identity, Jazz, and the Religious Compositions of Mary Lou Williams

Tammy Lynn Kernodle

The question of liturgical reform and renewal within the Catholic Church dominated ecclesiastical discussions in the 1960s. As early as the late 1950s, various important questions as to the necessity of updating the liturgy and church practices to reflect its changing physicality had been raised within the Church. However, it became apparent that one issue would not be answered easily: How could the liturgy be reformed without breaking with Church traditions?

Over time the Vatican itself addressed these concerns and attempted to bring some form of resolution. The Second Vatican Council, convened from 1962 until 1965, addressed two main issues that were particularly significant for American Catholics: the *Declaration on Religious Freedom* and the *Constitution on the Sacred Liturgy*. Although the council did not dictate a set of provisions to be carried out by the laity, it did signal the beginning of a period of significant liturgical changes within the Church and corresponding debates. This new liturgical era would ignite a progressive musical movement that integrated various musical styles with liturgical forms and altered the performance and composition of music within the Catholic Church.

The changes in the music used in worship services were reflected, most evidently, in the texts, musical styles, and instrumentation used in the Mass. Reformative acts during the post–Vatican II years raised questions within the Church: What is appropriate music for use in worship services? How far is too far in attempting to increase the accessibility of the liturgy? Unfortunately, these issues would not be easily resolved and both sides of the "reformative coin" would strongly disagree. There arose during this time an interesting dichotomy. While some parishes experimented with different approaches in worship music, others continued to use traditional chants in their services. Composers of church music divided themselves into compositional "camps" denoting their approaches to genre. Notable are the compositional approaches that "new" composers took to (writing) sacred music. Some used the official translations of the *Roman Missal* approved by the International Committee on English in the Liturgy (ICEL), while others translated liturgical material in contemporary contexts. Gregorian chant melodies were sometimes used with these contemporary scriptural interpretations, but others looked to musical sources outside of the Roman rite. The inclusion of folk, rock, and jazz elements into Mass settings called for new forms of instrumentation to be used in churches. Thus, the instrumentation used in the Catholic churches went beyond the traditional organist or pianist. Although Protestant churches had long included guitars, drums, and other instruments into their worship services, these instruments had rarely, if ever, been used in Catholic worship services.[1]

Despite the separation between traditionalists and reformers, it was obvious that the practice of composing and performing music within the Catholic Church would never be the same. The inclusion of musical forms outside of the Roman rite in worship services symbolizes more than the transition of the Mass from being exclusionary to inclusionary; it also represents the acknowledgment, whether consciously or subconsciously, of a cultural heritage that had largely been ignored by the Catholic Church. This is quite evident in the development and cultivation of the jazz Mass and the use of gospel music in various Catholic churches.

Jazz, blues, and gospel have since their beginnings been linked primarily with the African American community. For most Americans they have served as a musical documentation of the life experiences of African Americans and a strong representation of their cultural identity. The impact of the inclusion of these forms in Catholic worship services is twofold. First, the integration of African American musical forms into the liturgy provides the Church with identifying qualities that can be linked with the community of Blacks within the Church, which I refer to as the "Invisible Church within the Church." These are the Black clergy and laity who, until recently, have largely been ignored by the larger Church but have remained loyal to the Catholic faith.[2] Second, this act of inclusion validates, for promoters of a Black liturgy, the need for such cultural rituals within the Church. The inclusion of African American musical forms in worship services during the 1960s and 1970s was a continuation of the efforts of Black Catholics throughout the late nineteenth and early twentieth centuries to create their own identifiable religious services but maintain Catholic Church order. For Protestant African Americans this had not been a concern as they had long developed musical forms and worship practices that reflected their culture. Evidence indicates that as early

1. J. Michael Joncas, "Reforming and Renewing the Music of the Roman Rite," *Pastoral Music* (August/September 1994): 30–32.

2. The history of Black Catholics in the United States has recently been addressed in the publications of various scholars, including Father Cyprian Davis, Cecilia Moore, Diane Morrow and others. Cyprian Davis' work, *The History of Black Catholics in the United States* (New York: Crossroad Publishing Company, 1990), is held as the landmark text on the subject.

as the 1930s and 1940s, African American Catholics had begun "africanizing" the liturgy through combinations of liturgical text and spiritual melodies.

> The only effort that I know of, that attempted . . . to bring together black culture and Catholic worship within the United States were the efforts of a particular religious sister from somewhere, I believe, in Oklahoma. She attempted to cover the language of the Latin Mass with unadapted melodies from Negro spirituals. I remember the Kyrie was sung to the exact tune of "Nobody Knows the Trouble I See." The melody was an ill fitting garment for the works, however noble the idea behind the effort; the effect itself was less than successful.[3]

Thus the years preceding Vatican II should be viewed as years of conception, the 1960s and 1970s as the period of gestation, and the subsequent years as the period of fruition.

The concept of a Black liturgy was not fully realized until the emergence of Father Clarence Joseph Rivers. Best known for his efforts in revitalizing American Catholic music, Rivers ignited this push within the Black community with his first composition, "God is Love" and then the publication of the *American Mass Program*. Written in 1963, the *American Mass Program* combined Black spirituals with Gregorian chants. Despite the popularity of the work and the reforms of Vatican II, many leaders of the Church were still hesitant to embrace the use of a "Black liturgy." In some instances parishes rejected the use of spirituals in worship services, claiming that they were secular not sacred forms.[4] Nevertheless, Black Catholics continued to advocate liturgies reflecting their African heritage. As Rivers and his supporters pushed fervently toward the acknowledgment of Black Catholics, another lesser-known composer within the Church was working toward a similar cause.[5]

Jazz pianist Mary Lou Williams, who had converted to Catholicism in 1957, had by 1962 begun composing sacred works displaying a strong musical connection between the liturgy, jazz, and blues. These compositions, ranging in date from 1962 to 1970, were the product of the pianist's desire to create forms of jazz that would speak to younger generations and provide "healing for the soul." This body of works, consisting of hymns and Masses, displayed a unique combination of secular stylistic forms and sacred liturgy. More importantly these works were a continuation of Mary Lou Williams' desire to educate audiences about the importance and sanctity of jazz. For supporters of liturgical reform, who actively sought such combinations, these compositions validated their pursuit of reform. This essay documents the social and

---

3. Jon Michael Spencer, *Black Hymnody: A Hymnological History of the African American Church* (Knoxville: University of Tennessee Press, 1992), 184. For additional information see Sister Thea Bowman, "The Gift of African-American Sacred Song," in *Lead Me, Guide Me: The African American Catholic Hymnal* (Chicago: G.I.A. Publications, 1987).

4. Spencer, *Black Hymnody*, 189.

5. Rivers writes about the creation of a Black liturgy and the importance of music in worship services in *The Spirit in Worship* (Cincinnati: Stimuli, 1978) and *Soulfull Worship* (Cincinnati: Stimuli, 1974).

*Mary Lou Williams prior
to her conversion to
Catholicism. (Courtesy of
the Institute of Jazz Studies,
Rutgers University, Newark,
New Jersey.)*

musical agents that lead to this unique marriage between jazz and the Catholic liturgy. It discusses the importance of Vatican II in the development of musical forms reflective of a Black heritage. Although I take into account the historical efforts of Father Rivers, I will primarily focus on the genesis, performance, and theological and musical perspectives of the sacred compositions of jazz pianist Mary Lou Williams.

Born Mary Scruggs on 10 May 1910, Mary Lou Williams had a successful career as a jazz pianist and arranger that spanned every major stylistic trend of the genre. In the 1920s she began playing for various vaudeville troupes that passed through Pittsburgh, Pennsylvania. Later she joined the Theater Owners Booking Association, the main performance circuit for Black vaudeville talent in the 1920s and married baritone saxophonist John Williams. In the 1930s she followed Williams to Kansas City, Missouri, where she became immersed in the progressive and active jazz scene of the city. She would become a member of Andy Kirk's Twelve Clouds of Joy, one of the premiere territorial bands of the southwestern jazz scene, and become one of the most recognizable pianists and composers of the era. The 1940s were punctuated with solo recordings, performances, and arranging stints with Benny Goodman, Jimmie Lunceford, and Duke Ellington. She became one of the leading supporters of beboppers Thelonious Monk, Charlie Parker, and Dizzy Gillespie, opening her apartment to the young musicians and offering them her musical wisdom.

However, at the height of her career in 1954, Mary Lou walked off the stage of a Paris nightclub and vowed never to play again. The European jazz scene, inconsistency in employment, and the deaths of musicians Garland Wilson and Charlie Parker had exasperated and deeply affected the pianist, who had been working professionally since the age of twelve. Her despondency became debilitating and she retreated to her home in New York; she "prayed constantly" and read all of the Psalms because they "cooled [her] and made [her] feel protected."[6] She attempted during this period to separate herself from the jazz scene and repeated her vow never to play again. The next three years would consist of her converting to Catholicism, converting her New York apartment into a halfway house and/or soup kitchen for ailing musicians, and creating the Bel Canto Foundation to offer assistance to the needy. Her conversion and the personal relationships she cultivated with various priests eventually lead to her addressing her love for jazz and its conflict with her spirituality. Although initially reluctant to return to the jazz scene, Mary Lou did return to performing full-time in the 1960s, realizing that it might bring resolution to the conflict between her love for the music and her spiritual beliefs. Under the guidance of Father Anthony Woods, S.J., parish priest at St. Francis Xavier in New York, and Jesuit seminarian Peter O' Brien, Mary Lou embarked on a new form of jazz composition that would combine traditional jazz and blues with sacred texts.

The genre of sacred jazz, or as Mary Lou described it, "jazz for healing," would not only bring jazz to audiences who previously might have shunned it but introduced a new generation of listeners to the music of Mary Lou Williams. The concept that the sacred influenced jazz was nothing new, as some jazz artists of the 1950s hard bop and gospel jazz movements had looked to the Black church for musical inspiration. Duke Ellington, as early as the 1960s, had also begun experimenting with sacred compositions. None of these artists, however, were attempting to integrate jazz into the Catholic liturgy.

Although Mary Lou Williams does not hold the distinction of composing the first jazz Mass (Father Rivers' work preceded Williams'), she would establish a significant place in jazz and religious history. The theological and musical implications of these compositions were tremendous. First, the inclusion of jazz in worship services would further the efforts of Black Catholics to integrate into the Church musical forms that were reflective of their cultural traditions. Unfortunately, this would not come to fruition until the late 1980s with the publication of the hymnal *Lead Me, Guide Me: The African American Catholic Hymnal*. Second, the popularity of this genre could possibly resuscitate interest in jazz, which was waning after the death of John Coltrane. One must, however, not view the composition of sacred jazz as an oxymoron. Historically and musically, despite the assertions of many, there is a strong connection

---

6. Mary Lou Williams as quoted in Linda Dahl, *Morning Glory: A Biography of Mary Lou Williams* (New York: Pantheon Books, 2000), 240.

between Black secular and sacred forms. The only difference in many cases is the places where these genres are cultivated.[7]

The work of Clarence Rivers raised questions as to the appropriateness of jazz in Catholic worship services, but no definitive answer emerged. Supporters and critics continued to debate the issue as Williams began working on her first composition, "A Hymn in Honor of St. Martin de Porres." Williams' composition was inspired by the canonization of Martin de Porres in 1962, who was often referred to as "the Black Christ of the Andres." This appealed deeply to Mary Lou, as she battled with validating her African heritage within a mostly White denomination. She is even said to have recounted stories of being visited by the saint.[8] His canonization would also be her impetus for creating a body of sacred jazz compositions. Father Anthony Woods, close friend and religious confidant of Williams, remarked that he saw her as an "apostle in the musical world. Jazz and Catholicism are in harmony with her. Jazz is an expression of the American Negro culture, and it has something beautiful to offer the Church in the way of music."[9] "A Hymn in Honor of St. Martin de Porres" reflects the pianist's early compositional style, which is defined essentially by the use of a complex harmonic language. It is written for an expanded choir (each voice group doubled) and is primarily *a cappella* except for a short piano interlude in the midsection of the piece. The text, written by Woods, details the humanitarian efforts of Martin de Porres.

> St. Martin de Porres. His shepherd staff a dusty broom.
> St. Martin de Porres. The poor made a shrine of his tomb.
> St. Martin de Porres. He gentled creatures tame and wild.
> St. Martin de Porres. He sheltered each unwanted child.
>
> This man of love [God] born of the flesh, yet of God.
> This humble man healed the sick, raised the dead.
> His hand is quick
>
> To feed beggars and sinners. The starving homeless, and the stray.
>
> Oh, Black Christ of the Andes.
> Come feed and cure us now we pray.
>
> Oh, help us spare, oh Lord.
> Spare thy people, lest you be angered with me forever.

---

7. Mary Lou discusses her feelings on the spiritual elements of jazz in several sources, but the most descriptive discussion can be found in Lowell D. Holmes and John W. Thomson, *Jazz Greats Getting Better with Age* (New York: Holmes and Meier, 1986), 36. The relationship between blues and spirituals is discussed in James Cone, *The Spirituals and Blues: Interpretation* (New York: Da Capo Press, 1962).

8. Dahl, *Morning Glory,* 273.

9. Father Anthony Woods as quoted in Dahl, *Morning Glory*, 273.

This man of love born of the flesh, yet of God.
This humble man healed the sick, raised the dead.
His hand is quick.

St. Martin de Porres.[10]

Mary Lou intended for the revenue generated by the performance of the work to fund her struggling Bel Canto Foundation, but it yielded no profits.[11] Further dismaying was the reaction to the composition. The reviews were mixed, with some claiming that it was "neither fish not foul," not good "liturgical music nor good jazz," and "a blues stripped of its accent." [12] Despite the response Williams continued to compose hymns. These works began to indicate a significant change in her compositional approach, from the complex harmonic structure heard in "St. Martin de Porres," to simple but emotional vocal lines that could be sung by the average singer. One such work, "Anima Christi," a hymn written in 1963, is based on a twelve-bar blues played by piano, bass clarinet, and guitar. It employs a sound similar to the traditional gospel style of the '50s and early '60s with its use of call and response between the lead vocalist and the choir, accompanied by the recurring motive played by the instruments. It is a simple but effective musical formula.

The appeal of "Anima Christi," subsequent hymns, and the successful 1966 Carnegie Hall concert called "Praise the Lord in Many Voices," provided the pianist with the confidence to compose a jazz Mass. By 1970 she had not only completed four Masses, but had received a commission from the Vatican and had a ballet choreographed to the music of one of the Masses. These four works indicated Williams' approach to setting sacred liturgy over time, her own interpretation of these traditional texts, and her developing identity as a Black Catholic.

The first Mass, simply called *Mass* or the *Pittsburgh Mass,* was written in 1967, while Mary Lou was teaching at Seton High School in Pittsburgh. Mary Lou described the process as follows:

> Several priests who were jazz fans had been urging me to write a Mass. So I began composing one during the class. I'd tell kids to take a break and I'd write eight bars of the Mass. They'd sing it right off. Whenever the nuns came into the room, I'd shift to theory. But I wrote the Mass in a week.[13]

---

10. Mary Lou Williams, "St. Martin de Porres." The uncatalogued works of Mary Lou Williams (Newark, N.J.:The Institute of Jazz Studies, Rutgers University).

11. The composition debuted in November of 1962 at St. Francis Xavier Church in New York. Later Mary Lou recorded the hymn on the album *Jazz for the Soul.* Here the composition is called "Black Christ of the Andes." For more information see Marshall Peck, "Jazz Hymn to Honor Negro Saint," *New York Herald Tribune,* Oct. 1962.

12. Dahl, *Morning Glory,* 276.

13. John S. Wilson, "Mary Lou takes her Jazz Mass to Church," *New York Times,* 9 Feb. 1975.

Mary Lou Williams as liturgical jazz pianist. (Courtesy of the Institute of Jazz Studies, Rutgers University, Newark, New Jersey.)

It was performed in July of the same year at St. Paul's Cathedral. The performance consisted of a choir of thirteen participants drawn from a summer camp, accompanied by piano only. The Mass was received enthusiastically. Williams, however, discarded the composition, claiming it was "long, drawn out, like a symphony, like the kind of thing they have in churches." [14]

The second Mass, entitled *Mass for Lenten Season,* was written in 1968 and performed for six Sundays during Lent at St. Thomas the Apostle in New York, the mother church of the Paulist Fathers.[15] The third composition, *A Mass for Peace,* was the result of a commission from the Vatican in 1969. During that year Mary Lou completed a five-month engagement in Copenhagen and stopped in Rome on her way back to the United States. During a visit to the Vatican, Mary Lou met with several Church officials who took interest in her approach to sacred music. One such meeting resulted in a commission to write a new Mass for peace. [16] Williams completed the Mass by

14. Wilson, "Mary Lou takes her Mass."
15. Ibid.
16. Mary Lou Williams, *Music for Peace* (Mary Records), liner notes.

July and performed it at the Holy Family Church in Harlem for the memorial service of assassinated Kenyan leader Tom Mboya.[17]

The fourth Mass is the result of Williams' rescoring the *Mass for Peace.* Retitled *Mary Lou's Mass,* this is the best known of the four Masses and shows a kinship to the popular jazz rock idioms of the '60s and '70s. In a 1975 interview Williams asserted that she "decided to put it [the Mass] into a completely different jazz rock idiom and called upon a top-talented arranger, Bob Banks to help [her] in this unfamiliar field."[18] The result is a twelve-movement work that integrates jazz, blues, gospel, and Gregorian chant and material from the previous Masses. The Mass opens with the antiphon "The Lord Says"; the text is taken from Jer 29:11–12, 14. Following the "Act of Contrition," which is taken from the *Pittsburgh Mass,* the "Kyrie" begins. Williams did not musically set an English translation of the Latin text but used a contemporary version written by liturgist Robert Ledogar. The text reads as follows:

> For our lack of hope, Lord have mercy.
> For our lack of faith, Lord have mercy.
> For our failure to care, Lord have mercy.
>
> For letting ourselves be paralyzed with fear, Lord have mercy.
> For our divisions, Christ have mercy.
> For our jealousies, Christ have mercy.
>
> For our hatred, Lord have mercy.
> For not being peacemakers, Lord have mercy.
> For our lies, Lord have mercy on my soul.[19]

The "Kyrie" employs a rhythmic bass and piano line that supports the call and response performance between the soloist and choir. The "Gloria" is followed by the hymn "Lazarus," which was written specifically for the Ailey production and recording of *Mary Lou's Mass.* This hymn is a setting of Christ's parable of the beggar Lazarus and the rich man and is written for a solo voice. The responsorial psalm, "In His Days," segues into the "Alleluia," which is followed by the "Credo." The offertory, "Turn Aside from Evil," is a three-section work that begins with the antiphon "Turn Aside from Evil." It then segues into a short recitation of the "Sanctus," which is followed by an eight-measure improvised bossa nova. The movement ends with a return to "Turn Aside from Evil." The "Our Father" is a combination of the text and the antiphon "Blessed are the Peace Makers" from the *Mass for Peace.* The "Agnus Dei" is

---

17. Mboya was assassinated in July of 1969.

18. Wilson, "Mary Lou takes her Mass."

19. Mary Lou Williams (score) and Robert Ledogar (words), "Kyrie" (Lord Have Mercy), in *Mary Lou's Mass.* The uncatalogued works of Mary Lou Williams. (Newark, N.J.: Institute of Jazz Studies, Rutgers University).

in traditional chant practice with the basses sustaining a low F pedal while the upper male voices recite the chant melody. This is the only piece within the Mass that makes reference to traditional worship music. Following the antiphon, "People in Trouble," which speaks to the ills of society and imminent destruction without repentance, the Mass ends with the jubilant hymn "Praise the Lord."[20]

This revised version of the *Mass for Peace* was inspired by choreographer Alvin Ailey, who had used spirituals and gospel music in previous works such as "Revelations" (1960) and had recently worked with Leonard Bernstein on his *Mass.* Mary Lou had considered the possibilities of combining the music of the Mass with dance, but felt that Ailey would not be interested. However, Ellington's sacred concerts and Bernstein's Mass had opened the way for such a collaboration. The result was *Mary Lou's Mass,* a Mass and ballet that combined elements of the ordinary and proper that corresponded with church order. The work premiered on 9 December 1971. Reviews were mixed. One reviewer asserted that "despite the genuineness of its emotion and devotion, the piece—scored for singers, French horn, drums, Conga, bass and reeds—lacks character, particularly melodic character."[21] The review in *Dance Magazine* described the performance as follows:

> These dances of supplication, repentance, fellowship, and exultation reveal the spirit, if not the essence of the liturgical celebration. The work has a ring of truth (and biblical precedent behind it) powerful enough to bring back an agnostic into the fold. . . . There are passages of *Mary Lou's Mass* as memorable as those in Ailey's earlier go at the spiritual in dance, his masterwork, "Revelations." The Kyrie chant, with its African beat that draws forth a pulsating orgy of arm and head movements. The Gloria, with its hoppity shouts of praise for the Lord, arms pricking the air, or the Sanctus, girls rustling their skirts with a warm sensualness, and the boys saying hosanna with a jazz dance. . . . Dancers, singers, and musicians, too numerous to name did Ailey and Williams proud.[22]

The work continued to be performed as a part of Ailey's repertoire until 1973. The Ailey ballet and the accompanying music led to the re-release of the original recording of *Mass for Peace* (1971) but with the additional movements. In 1975 Mary Records, named for the Virgin Mary and owned by Williams, released the recording as *Mary Lou's Mass.*

During the 1970s, Mary Lou continued to perform the work in churches and schools across the country, each time rescoring the piece to fit their vocal abilities. She main-

---

20. For a more detailed discussion of each movement of the Mass see Tammy L. Kernodle *"Anything You Are Shows Up in Your Music": Mary Lou Williams and the Sanctification of Jazz* (Ph.D. diss., Ohio State University, 1997).

21. Review of performance of *Mary Lou's Mass,* by Mary Lou Williams and Alvin Ailey, Alvin Ailey American Dance Theater, *Hi/Fi America* (1972): MA15.

22. Review of performance of *Mary Lou's Mass,* by Mary Lou Williams and Alvin Ailey, Alvin Ailey American Dance Theater, *Dance Magazine* (Feb. 1972): 26.

tained these activities through the efforts of her manager, Jesuit seminarian and later priest, Peter O'Brien. His relationship with Williams was unique. He was her full-time manager and one of many associate priests at St. Ignatius Loyola Church in New York. O'Brien asserts that "[He] was full time with her and full time with the Jesuits. The Jesuits are very flexible and [he] was authorized to travel with her and help with her career. This would have been much more difficult for [him] in any other organization within the Church." [23]

Williams and O'Brien conducted jazz history workshops throughout the country during the 1970s. These workshops generally consisted of O'Brien presenting an outline of the evolution of jazz and Mary illustrating various examples on the piano, concluding with performances by local choirs of *Mary Lou's Mass*.[24] In addition to touring and lecturing, Mary Lou once again returned to the New York jazz scene, where she gained a new generation of listeners. For the first time in almost twenty years, Williams was once again being recognized for her unquestionable musical talent. Smaller independent record labels courted her for recording dates. Hoping to use this attention to increase exposure for sacred jazz music, she pushed to record religious music, but the lack of interest diverted her toward traditional jazz styles.

Still determined to continue her efforts in creating music that would reflect her spirituality, Mary Lou looked to performing *Mary Lou's Mass* in St. Patrick's Cathedral in New York. Considering it to be not "proper protocol" to initiate such a request, Father O'Brien declined to ask Cardinal Terence Cooke. Mary Lou cornered the cardinal and asked about the possibilities of performing the Mass. He was enthusiastic, but many at St. Patrick's were not ready to deal with the notion of jazz in a church setting. Four years would pass before the idea of performing the Mass was seriously considered.

In 1975 Monsignor James F. Rigney, rector of the cathedral, wrote to the principals of the New York Catholic high schools, because he wanted the schoolchildren to feel that they had a claim on the cathedral. Thomas Murphy, S.J., president of Regis High School, suggested that *Mary Lou's Mass* be given for the children.[25] Mary Lou agreed not only to perform the Mass but also to include the students in the performance. She rescored the vocal lines and trained a choir of forty students from the grammar school of Our Lady of Lourdes, Fordham Prep in the Bronx, and the Cathedral High School for Girls in Manhattan.[26] John Donohue, reviewer for *America* magazine, wrote of the performance as follows:

> On February 18, 1975 some 200 people filled St. Patrick's Cathedral all eager to hear *Mary Lou's Mass*. At 2:10 p.m., the concelebrants of the Mass filed in, announced by exciting chords and dazzling arpeggios from the piano, and the liturgy began. For it was,

23. O'Brien as quoted in Dahl, *Morning Glory*, 314.

24. Dahl, *Morning Glory,* 314. Mary Lou is known to have rescored the Mass in each performance to fit the voice ranges of the participants. This has resulted in numerous versions of the Mass.

25. Wilson, "Mary Lou takes her Mass."

26. Ibid.

first of all, a liturgy and not just a performance. The readings set that Tuesday, the first week of Lent, were done by Miss Williams' friend Mabel Mercer. Msgr. James F. Rigney, the rector of the cathedral, had some graceful words of welcome, and then Fr. O'Brien preached a moving homily echoing the theme Miss Williams had touched upon a week before—the parallel roles of suffering in the life of our Lord and in the lives of black composers of jazz. [27]

Accompanied by a bassist, drummer, and choir of one hundred students from local Catholic high schools and from the State University at Purchase, Mary Lou Williams became the first jazz composer to perform at St. Patrick's Cathedral. The response was overwhelming and Williams responded by stating that "Americans don't realize how important jazz is. It's healing to the soul. It should be played *everywhere*—in churches, night clubs, everywhere. We have to use it every place we can."[28]

Central to this discussion is the impact and importance of the Second Vatican Council and the subsequent reforms within the Church. Although Vatican II did not provide specific instructions for reforms such as new music for the liturgy, it did provide the environment for discourse and experimentation. In the years following Vatican II various documents addressed the issue of liturgical reform. In 1967 the Sacred Congregation for Rites issued *Musicam Sacram*, which provided instruction for the normal use of music in worship services. In 1972 the Bishop's Committee on Liturgy of the United States Catholic Conference published the edict "Music in Catholic Worship," which established the norms and priorities for the selections of music in worship services.[29] These guidelines would appear two years after the composition and performance of Mary Lou's final Mass and would suggest many of the compositional approaches that she had used. However, it is important to note that by 1972 the movement of incorporating new forms of music in worship services was well under way with the performance of folk Masses, rock Masses, and jazz Masses in churches. One cannot help wondering if Mary Lou's Masses served as the archetype for the provisions expressed in "Music in Catholic Worship," or if the performance of *Mary Lou's Mass* in St. Patrick's Cathedral was the litmus test for these new provisions. The sources available reveal neither. What is known is that Mary Lou Williams, through scripture-based texts blended with jazz harmonies and rhythms, had gained the favor of the Vatican, gained the ears of a new generation of listeners, and provided another dimension to the emerging identity of Black Catholics in the late twentieth century.

---

27. John Donohue, "'Mary Lou's Mass': Music for Peace," *America* (March 8, 1975).

28. Peter Keepnew, "Liturgy of Jazz at St. Patrick's," *New York Post* (19 Feb. 1975).

29. "Music in Catholic Worship and Liturgical Music Today," *The Liturgy Document: A Parish Resources*, rev. ed., ed. Mary Ann Sincoe (Chicago: Chicago Liturgy Training Publication, 1985).

Freeing the Spirit: Very Personal Reflections on One Man's Search for the Spirit in Worship

Clarence-Rufus J. Rivers

Prologue

> Brothers and Sisters in Christ: Although some sayings
> may be hard for us to hear and bear, we have been told
> to be open to the liberating truth. And the truth is
> that worship in most of our churches, most of the time,
> is dull and uninspiring. Whereas the worshiping congregation
> should be a dramatic dance life, instead it is all too often
> like the dry bones in the vision of Ezekiel, a static, stagnant sprawl
> of lifeless limbs, a tableau of death. We seem to be there merely
> physically, not really hearing anything that moves us, not
> saying anything that moves others. Our faith would seem to
> make us exuberant proclaimers of the Joy of Life. But we
> appear deaf and dumb, unmoved and unmoving. We do not
> seem to be God's chosen people, rather God's frozen people.
> And to the extent that we appear deaf and dumb and dead and
> lifeless, to that extent we are not witnesses for everlasting life, but
> witnesses for never-ending death.

Cold Worship: Our Starting Point

Our Ancestors's Reaction to Cold Worship

Our fore parents, when allowed to attend the worship services of those who enslaved them, *found the worship incomplete.* They would remain in the churchyard afterwards and would form a circle and dance until they felt possessed by the Spirit of God.

My Grandmother's Reaction to Cold Worship

Many generations later, my maternal grandmother, Eugenia Houser Echols, used to say how much she admired the charitable works of the Catholic Church, when finally there was a Catholic presence in the Black community of Selma. She told over and over again how this Catholic nun rolled back layers and layers of skirt, like an onion, and got down on her bare knees to scrub the splintered floor of this sick and aged colored woman. My grandmother had never before witnessed a White person serving, in a menial capacity, the needs of a colored person. She was impressed, and even in the retelling of the story her voice took on all the emotion, all the surprise and her own joy-filled enthusiasm that she had first felt when witnessing this Sister of St. Joseph performing corporal works of mercy. Eugenia was always on fire during the telling of this marvelous narrative and would always, reaching for the strongest notes in her speaking voice, exclaim and proclaim: "If there ever was a Christian, he was a CA—THO—LIC!!!" Moreover, she enjoyed the humane blend of ritual movement, color, and pageantry, the dignified drape of vesture, and the provocative and evocative smell of incense in Catholic worship. But when someone asked her why she was not a Catholic, she answered, almost-not-quite shivering, "Their worship is much too cold." There was the slightest hint of regret in her voice.[1]

For her and most Blacks (and, I believe, "for most people"), Catholic worship lacks the warmth and fire of the "HOLY GHOST." It is not inspiring. Our worship did not leave my grandmother spiritually fulfilled; it left her spiritually unfed. It did not move her beyond admiration of the vesture and the rites of the Church to the ardent fervor of spiritual growth and continuing conversion.

Pope Paul VI's Reaction to Cold Worship

It would be a mistake to think that the spiritual vitality sought by my grandmother was a cultural phenomenon inherited uniquely out of her African/African American

---

1. To tell the truth the Reformed Presbyterian Church of Selma was nothing to brag about; the church home of the Echols family disallowed the playing of the organ and piano on the Sabbath—i.e. Sunday. That was servile work! I remember my mother agonizing over her dilemma of what sin to commit: should she sew her stockings on Sunday so she could go to church, or should she miss church because she had no stockings to wear? I could have been no more than four or five years old at the time; all of my "judgments" must have come much later. The Echols' were sedate, upper class and impoverished; the Rivers' were lower-class Baptists but economically fared much better. The Reformed Presbyterian Church of Selma, as I have seen it as an adult, was a run down wooden structure on Jeff Davis Avenue almost tucked out of sight, but Tabernacle Baptist was a fine yellow brick structure with some style on the main thoroughfare, Broad Street. The former was a missionary church, partially supported from the outside (from up North), with a pastor sent from elsewhere; the latter was a self-supporting congregation who hired its own pastor. My grandmother was more in spirit a Black Baptist; after all, she was by birth a Houser, not an Echols.

background. Eugenia Houser Echols's needs were also the needs of Europeans, because they are human needs. It is simply that European/European American Catholics feel a bit squeamish, a bit guilty, criticizing anything that is of the Church. On the other hand, in the glaring light of the massive defections of cradle Catholics of Central and South America to the churches of fundamentalist missionaries, Pope Paul VI—in a letter to the Bishop's Conference of Latin America (CELAM)—wrote that "worship which did not move the congregation inspirationally, nor lead them to continuing conversion, could not be considered authentic."

The Average European American's Reaction to Cold Worship

But more telling than any official statement is the *reaction* of "grass root" folks in the Church. I remember attending a service of carols with a group of people from a dinner party. The music started out being charming, even enchanting. However, the carols showed no vitality, and every song began to sound like the previous ones; this group merely endured the service for the more than two hours it took to run its course. Back in the hostess' sitting room, this group could not overcome its Catholic upbringing and dare to criticize the service of carols directly. In fact, they never mentioned once the event that had brought them together for the evening and that had bored them to death. But, tellingly, the conversation went immediately to limiting the time that a Mass should take: one half hour or less was ideal, and forty five minutes was the absolute maximum. This was the way that a majority of Catholics (outside the Black community) expressed their dissatisfaction with their liturgy—when they come to the table of the Lord to be spiritually fed, but instead are left spiritually hungry and *even angry* at the broken promise, which offers them, in theory, life, but instead bores them to death. It is no chance phenomenon that the stampede away from Sunday Mass is one of the fastest and angriest movements in the life of the average Catholic. One might say that the catalyst for the impatience and anger is the traffic congestion when parking is at a premium, but one might be wrong. For the anger and impatience before Mass is not so ferocious as it is after Mass.

The Beginning of a Professional Liturgist

Pastoral Encouragement

As a newly ordained minister (1956) and associate pastor to Msgr. Clement J. Busemeyer at St. Joseph's Parish in the West End of Cincinnati, I expected this exteriorly gruff, teutonic pastor to be unconcerned about the *quality* of worship; his masses took from twenty to thirty minutes, the "sacred words" slovenly raced over in the widespread custom of the day. However, he was very much concerned that worship was not reaching and touching the people in the pews. One day he said to me, "People are coming to church only because they're afraid of *catching hell*, if they don't!" He then pointedly asked, "Can you do something about this?" His clumsy question is much more vivid in memory than my crazy response, which, I believe, was an unequivocal, though naïve, "Yes, I think I can! I can do something about THIS!"

My response, in the clear light of looking back, was not as ambitious as the words would seem to indicate. In presiding at Mass, usually the main parish Mass, I would intensify my efforts to read the Latin texts so as to convey their meaning. There was no illusion that the people would understand the Latin, but they must see that I, for the most part, did understand and was more or less raptured by my understanding. There was a certain validity in presuming that they could be moved by experiencing that I was moved. However, they must understand their own responses, and they must convey the meaning in the English hymns, psalms, and songs, to themselves and to one another. That was not to ask a great deal for the moment, and it laid a basis for further development.

Beginning to Compose

Fr. Busemeyer had also indicated that he saw a place for Black music in the Catholic Church. He lamented the fact that the archbishop had not allowed a concert of Negro spirituals at the (not yet restored) cathedral. My own interpretation of this was that there should be a place for all Black religious culture in worship. Around the same time Fr. Boniface Luykx, a Belgian Norbertine monk, on his way going to or coming from his annual courses in liturgy taught at Notre Dame, began to stop off in Cincinnati. On one occasion he challenged Giles Harry Pater, a very dear friend of mine, and me to start composing music for the liturgy out of our own backgrounds. There was nothing wrong with challenging Harry; he was a trained, educated musician. But there was a danger in challenging me: I did not know enough to know that I could not compose. Or closer to the truth, I really believed that musical compositions, especially with words, must be as natural as speaking a language even before becoming literate in that language. So I accepted the challenge.

I knew that a Sister of the Blessed Sacrament had set the text of *The Latin Ordinary of the Mass* to the tune of several Negro spirituals. The "Kyrie" was set to the tune of "Nobody Knows the Trouble I See." Though Sister's vision of introducing the power and pathos of African American music into worship was nothing less than commendable, I remember Charles Rehling suggesting that the results might have been more effective had she used the "elements" of the spirituals, instead of forcing whole, unchanged and undiluted melodies onto the Latin text, where they did not fit. Her efforts and Charles's comments were the only technical, critical preparation I had before rushing in past the nontreading Angels.

One Sunday afternoon I was returning from Virginia Beach where I had delivered a speech on race relations. I was not yet used to flying, and, I must say, Piedmont Airlines' little prop jet did not inspire confidence. We were flying over the Appalachian mountains during a thunderstorm. I needed to do something to take my mind off Piedmont's little prop jet and the thunderstorm. I took out my (before-its-time) English-language breviary and started to read the Sunday Office. I was struck with the words of

A young Clarence Rivers sings his own composition, "God is Love." (Courtesy of Clarence Rivers.)

St. John: "God is love; and he who abides in love abides in God; and God in him." I started applying a melody and a musical rhythm to the piece, mostly in my head, and possibly humming very softly to myself and occasionally scrawling lines and dots as pegs to my memory. I repeated the melody incessantly in my head. When I got back to St. Joseph's, I taught the melody to the Sisters of St. Francis (from Oldenburg) who taught in our school, who in turn taught the whole of the primary school to sing the refrain. Meanwhile, I had to compose verses and teach them to Phil Schoch and Joe Muldrow, our instantly created cantors. With one stroke, almost unconsciously, a change in American church music had begun.

But the way had already been prepared. Fr. Luykx had brought me a tape of the *Missa Luba*, which the sisters had taught to the primary school. One day, Msgr. Busemeyer had heard the children's lusty, robust singing of the Luba Mass as he strolled through the school. He returned to the rectory almost breathless with enthusiasm. He said that he had never heard the "Kyrie" and the "Sanctus" and other parts of the Mass Ordinary sung with such enthusiasm. Therefore, he asked, weren't we obliged to let the children sing this at Mass? Not entirely guileless I responded, "I guess so Father!" Msgr. Busemeyer insisted that the children sing the Luba Mass for his twenty-fifth ordination jubilee. The barn door had been left open! In due time, in rushed the spirituals, gospel, jazz, my occasional compositions, and all the rest. As I remarked earlier, a Cincinnati archbishop had forbidden a concert of Negro spirituals at the cathedral on the implausible and shaky grounds that they were "secular" songs, but by this time the patently implausible grounds were much too shaky to stand up under the potentially weighty charge of racism. Certainly, not even an archbishop would have risked his authority being tainted with the opprobrium of being politically incorrect.

However, music, from any source, whatever its vitality, could not and cannot carry the full weight of effective worship. In line with our pastoral mandate to improve worship and to encourage congregational vitality and responsiveness, I worked hard at improving my sermons. With hindsight, I know that my sermon efforts were not very moving, but in the homiletic desert of the times they were frequently "interesting" by reason of content and perspective. If in spite of strenuous effort I came up with nothing that was even interesting, I simply did not preach. I did not preach in spite of congregational encouragement to do so *anyhow*. The congregations figured, I think, that I was being modest and would have always had "something" of interest to say, but I knew that their confidence was misplaced. Moreover, I continued to feel the "urge" to make worship focused and coherent. Without the latter the total liturgy would not have its most intense impact and effect in spite of the fact that one or more parts might be individually effective.

My Co-Workers

Very few people get anything done without the intimate collaboration of others. My co-workers were the Sisters of Saint Francis from Oldenburg, Indiana. They always had the schoolchildren well prepared to participate in the main Sunday liturgy, and, when necessary, they prodded and disturbed my own inertia, reminding me: "You promised us a new communion hymn." It was not only the schoolchildren who had to be taught, however; the full congregation itself had to be taught to sing in a manner that was alive rather than dead and deadening. The entire congregation had to become collaborators and concelebrants,[2] and so, only half-vested, I came before the parish assembly before the main liturgy on Sunday morning. No matter how long it took, I reasoned that the Mass could not proceed until the primary witness of the faith, the worshiping assembly, was ready to express that faith. I tried to teach them to sing and respond with a vitality that betokened a living faith. I "threatened," cajoled, made fun of their bad singing habits, and encouraged them to repeat their best attempts. Not everybody could have gotten away with this outrage that I was perpetrating, but they loved me, and I knew that and took advantage of my place in their hearts. Moreover, and perhaps more profoundly, the congregation enjoyed succeeding. Gratefully, they started to give of themselves in a manner that was fitting, at least for the moment.

---

2. I have never accepted that demon of modern reform that took us a step backwards: calling only vested "ordained" priests concelebrants. Everybody knows that *orders*, a military term, crept into Christianity through a Greco-Roman general who become emperor and issued *orders*, military orders, to Christian elders to oversee his provinces (in Greek: dioceses) in order to keep the Roman aristocracy out of politics.

Nothing Succeeds Like Success

Keep in mind that this was happening before the Vatican Council's exhortations on congregational participation. So in spite of the fact that we did nothing to specifically advertise our parish liturgies, the Church started to have a few visiting strangers each Sunday, and that was encouraging. There were a few of our own parishioners, however, who could not stand the strain of active participation and took refuge in the pastor's twenty to thirty minute "quiet" Mass.

Msgr. Busemeyer wanted us to make the main liturgy spiritually alive. ("Spiritually alive" is redundant.) But for complex reasons, he continued the "quiet" Mass. Among other things, the pastor wanted a comparison, and those who were aware and capable of judging saw that the quiet Mass was not alive with silent prayer. Rather the quiet of this Mass was like that in the valley of Ezekiel's dry bones before the miracle. The sisters and I were not given to academic worship analysis. We never really discussed to any great extent, if at all, the things that made our Sunday worship moderately effective. We knew we were effective by an occasional comparison to the liturgies that we witnessed elsewhere. (Remember, there was not a great deal going on elsewhere until some time after the council.) Sometimes, it was the comment of an occasional visitor that helped label and categorize some of our efforts: "Your parish Mass seems to flow so smoothly." At the time, I felt the need to stitch together the sequential parts of the liturgy with a few discreet words taken from Scripture, songs, or simply poetic language taken from other literature. I did not realize it immediately, but I was feeling the need to keep worship from being static by giving it movement. Ultimately, I realized that all drama, including the drama of worship, needed movement from beginning to middle to end. The loose strings from various studies or from comments of professors started to be woven into a coherent pattern. Given a few years and a great deal of experience, I was beginning to understand how to plan a liturgy. It slowly dawned on me that a well-structured (aesthetically structured) worship was the same as a vitally effective, spiritually moving worship. Even this slow learner caught on eventually. Saint Joseph's parish was moving with moderate speed toward an effective worship and a more comprehensive idea of inculturation, i.e., synthesizing and integrating African American culture and Catholic worship. This was a matter more sophisticated and complex than adding a few Black-flavored hymns/songs onto an otherwise unyielding Roman rite.

Our schoolchildren at St. Joseph's were invited to other parishes, but this was getting us unwanted attention. When word finally reached the newspapers that there was "drumming" in St. Joseph's Church on Ezzard Charles's Drive, a letter came from the archbishop's office demanding that we use only "sacred instruments." But as I said before, the barn door was open! Some weeks after the receipt of that letter, Bishop Paul Leibold, who had written the "no secular instruments" letter at the mandate of Archbishop Karl Alter, was coming to St. Joseph's to administer the sacrament of Confirmation. Msgr. Busemeyer declared three evenings of preparation: (1) to explore the meaning of confirmation; (2) to practice the ceremonies; and (3) to prepare and invigorate the congregational participation—especially the music. Imagine pastors telling their congregations they have to turn out for all four evenings, three immediately prior to the evening of Confirmation and the evening of Confirmation itself. In those days, however, when Clement Busemeyer spoke, everyone (almost) listened and obeyed, for they respected and loved him because he was good to his people.

In our music preparations we were mainly using Gelineau psalm settings. We did not have an organist, so the schoolchildren borrowed my set of Ugandan drums. I said it was only for temporary use in rehearsing. In the back of my mind, however, I knew we had to have some instrument to help the congregation keep its ensemble. So I went to Purcell High School, where I taught, borrowed the timpani set, and snuck it up into the choir loft. When the procession stepped into church, I unleashed the energy of the schoolchildren on the timpani; the congregation sang with all their hearts. Msgr. Clement J. Busemeyer was seen patrolling the side aisles with a smile on his face that out-toothed the Cheshire Cat.

Bishop Leibold, when asked by an "unwise" young sister how he liked the music, very wisely avoided the subject (i.e., the mandate forbidding "non-sacred" instruments) and responded: "I'm for giving these people all the singing they can get." The local clergy were gathered there, as was the commendable custom *in diebus illis*—in comradeship and martinis. When I walked into the pastor's living room to join this clerical assembly, someone yelled across the room, "Hey Rivers, were these drums "liturgical"? (He meant " rubrical.") However, before I had a chance to respond, Msgr. Busemeyer intervened: "You know, five years ago you wouldn't have heard THAT." He too, like the bishop, avoided the subject. Moreover, Msgr. Busemeyer had the full understanding that I had, without his permission, put his "prestige" on the line by violating a direct order written to him by the bishop. If we had not succeeded, I might have gotten a tongue lashing. If one is going to violate orders for pastoral reasons, one had better succeed in the endeavor, making incarnate aesthetic and pastoral insight and thereby outweighing the "theory or abstraction" of legislated principle. I had gambled on that, and nothing more was ever said about THAT.

This foolish assistant pastor, with the dedicated collaboration of "unwise" Oldenburg Franciscan Sisters, had rushed in where angels feared to tread and had not been rebuked, nor reprimanded, nor scolded. Why? Because we had done it well. Armed only with naiveté, a little skill (in handling, teaching, and leading people), and a strong desire to make worship vital, we had gained (or always had) the allegiance of the congregation who sang their hearts out, and we found the results satisfying. The sisters and I had few abstract ideals to lead us. We were simply in love with incarnate, authentic, and vital worship. Even so we could only do what the pastor allowed us to do. Gratefully, he wanted what we wanted, so he allowed us what, in those days, was a great deal of freedom in handling parish worship. The result: we did much of what Vatican II would eventually encourage.[3]

---

3. In preparing worship, a pastor and his associates must sometimes accept that prudent risk taking can establish a new norm or overturn an old one. If the risk is taken, under controlled circumstances, then the

The sisters and I were products of our times. Therefore, we did not think of our attempts in worship as revolutionary; rather we were attempting to recapture what we thought was a forgotten tradition. We were full-time teachers who worked on worship—mainly on music and congregational participation—only in a "beginning" way. As I have acknowledged, without the prodding of the Oldenburg Franciscan Sisters, I would not have done as much as I did. Try as I will, I am unable to remember all of their names, but there are some partners in crime that I cannot forget: Sister Ephrem, Sister Christopher (Mary O'Brien), Sister Andre Burkhardt, and Sister Francesca Thompson.

The sisters and I worked from a musical base, not excluding other less obvious but vitally necessary elements. However, none of us were what the world would call musically expert (maybe Sr. Ephrem was the exception) or even literate. But on reflection I have not found this remarkable; as I often explained, "Our ancestors, who invented language, were not literate."

The Elements of Success: Proximate Preparation

Not By Music Alone

There should be one clarification about our use of music in worship. In my experience the kind of music was not as important as its effective delivery. I worked with the congregation before main liturgies, and they responded well. Backed up by the schoolchildren and prepared by the nuns, the congregation was able to sing and otherwise participate very actively in our communal worship. The distinction between the High Mass and the Low Mass began to fade before the decrees of Vatican II were ever promulgated. As I have previously touched on, I had always thought that our sermons should be worked on, written out, and written as poetically as possible. Above all I thought I had to have something worth saying, something that touched people. Otherwise I did not preach.

I also thought that the liturgy ought to have integrity and be a staged religious play, with its parts stitched together with embroidering threads of scripture text or song phrases—so that parts of the worship flowed naturally from one to another. I had not fully thought this out; I was simply acting from the instincts that made me very uncomfortable when presiding at worship when worship did not have the appropriate qualities that inspired the people. Without these qualities, I felt that worship was not only inappropriate, it was not really worship. Not being entirely a slow learner, moving

---

outcome is predictably a pastoral success. This is not a revolutionary thought. It is the prudent exercise of the virtue that we learned about in scholastic philosophy and traditional moral theology. Just about every change for real pastoral good can be found to be justified in traditional philosophy and theology. I simply do not know where I would be—existentially—without a broad knowledge of scholastic philosophy and theology. The tradition of Thomism (the broad principles of Thomas Aquinas) is very useful liturgically and otherwise.

at the speed of an opening flower petal, it dawned on me, as a fully articulated concept, that well-sung music was not sufficient for effective, authentic worship. The structure of worship must have unity and coherence. It must not be static; to move the congregation, worship itself had to move perceptibly from beginning to middle to end. It had to have the qualities that Aristotle discovered in effective drama.

It goes without saying that I felt a need to perform, to proclaim, to announce, and to pray as if I meant the texts that I was saying or singing. That is to say, I never felt comfortable unless I was habitually familiar with the texts of the missal (not yet divided into sacramentary, lectionary, and Gospel books), understood them, and delivered them with the appropriate understanding evident in my voice through pronunciation, enunciation, inflection, various pitches, pauses, and, sometimes, repetition.

Laying a Basis for Accomplishment: Remote Preparation Outside the Seminary

Even before I entered the seminary in the eleventh grade, I knew that I needed to learn to sing better, so I was on the lookout for voice training. Through the mediation of a friend, Dr. Eugene Orlando, a hot-headed and outrageously generous musician came all the way across town, from North Bend to the West End, to give this skinny little boy his first voice lessons. I only mention this to point out that my instincts were to prepare myself to be a fit instrument to preside at worship. I really did not think that anything else was as important as worship, but at the time I could not have fully articulated any of these feelings. I did not even know the *words*, let alone the *thought* of "presiding at worship."

What I did have was a love for ceremonials, which was absorbed unconsciously from my association with all of the "servers"/altar boys of St. Edward's–St. Ann's parish. The pastors and assistant pastors, from the time of Charles F. Murphy through the time of Arnold F. Witzman, taught us how to assist at all of the Church's rituals, and somehow they managed to teach us to love doing it well. As children we joked about being graceful, even in making mistakes. For example, we agreed that if we should find ourselves moving to the wrong position, we should not make a sudden stop and awkwardly backtrack, thereby betraying our mistake. Rather we should continue in the wrong direction until it seemed reasonable to stop; then we should turn slowly, pause for a count of six to ten, and only then should we return to our proper places without ever acting nervous or embarrassed or in any way that might cause the congregation to give us undue notice. We were prepared to serve in any position, from torchbearer, to acolyte, to master of ceremonies, and on occasion even the role of sub-deacon was afforded by observing the scruple of not wearing a maniple. We all loved being servers. Our grade school teachers, Sisters of the Blessed Sacrament, made sure that we knew our Latin responses. I am sure that a love of the liturgy was planted in those days, and that some of what I have called "instincts for good worship" were also planted there, long before any of us had discursive, conceptual thoughts about liturgy and public worship.

After experiencing the significance of literature, drama, and voice, I incorporated them into my understanding of the liturgy. In drama, including the drama of worship, not even gesture can be merely "real." In *Julius Caesar*, Cassius, in an angry exchange with Brutus, says, "Here my dagger and here my naked breast." Cassius draws his dagger, places it in front of Brutus, and bares his breast. The gesture of "drawing" cannot be simply laying his dagger in front of Cassius. The dagger must be seen by the audience, so Cassius must hold it high (just high enough to be seen), and only then may he place it before Brutus.

If the Sisters of St. Francis and I had some success in spite of our naiveté, it was because we came to the job prepared by our backgrounds and also with certain ideals about liturgy that we had picked up, somehow, along the way. We had no formal courses in worship. The closest that I had come to a formal course in worship was given by Fr. Ed Gratsch, and that was mainly a survey of the rubrics and laws governing worship. I do remember that Fr. Gratsch made us aware that not all rubrics and laws were matters of weighty or serious concern. That was—though he himself was not consciously aware of the fact—a matter of pastoral concern.

Freeing the Spirit

During the early 1960s invitations started to come in for our workshops in music and worship. I urged the sponsors of these workshops to allow seven to ten days for programming, which consisted of evening lectures on worship. Two hours each evening were devoted to learning the music, which was then used in a climactic concert and/or a Sunday morning Eucharist.

The intensive music rehearsals were not merely for the sake of the music. These rehearsal sessions were used to get across certain points about worship and performance in worship. For example, when the participants were tired and seemed not to have the energy to enter fully into the program of the evening, I used the occasion to disabuse them of the notion that in public worship we ought to communicate our personal feelings. I called that belief "the idolatry of sincerity," pointing out that on Easter Sunday the parish priest did not have the right to communicate his "hangover"; rather he must transcend his personal feeling in order to convey the hope and the joy of the Resurrection.

Another favorite "idol" was that liturgy ought to be "spontaneous," and that too much practice would make the performer in worship too stiff. Wrong again, I countered; too little practice makes one stiff and awkward. After years of grueling practice, a gymnast appears to do his/her routine effortlessly. Effortlessly, after years of practice!?! They would get the point! Then, I would say, you do not have to believe, but I want you to sing as if you did. All such ideas were handled casually and with as much wit and humour as I could summon.

If there were a lecture or concert scheduled, the lecture (basically a humorous monologue) was meant to break down their inhibitions, to allow the assembly to participate more freely, and to close up all of the little dark pigeon holes where people were wont to hide from active and vital participation in worship. Again, the musical portion of the evening was not an end in itself; it was a way of involving the entire assembly rather than letting them be onlookers and voyeurs in this love song that we sing to God, i.e., the liturgy.

In many cases the sponsors asked for just a weekend program. In this situation, I felt obliged to pack more talk and conversation into the all-day Saturday program than I would have liked to do, but I felt obligated to let pastors and people know about all the elements of a liturgy. I felt it would have been, at the very least, unfaithful on my part to leave people with the impression that music was the alpha and omega of worship. On the other hand, I did and do believe that the whole of the liturgy should be, in the deepest sense of the word, musical/poetic/dramatic. However, this would involve infinitely more than singing a few good songs at Mass.

Having said that, I must acknowledge that without my "new" music as bait I might never have had all the invitations to work in so many parishes and universities. Therefore, I might never have developed my liturgical skills, nor deepened my understanding of "what makes worship work." My fullest understanding came about slowly, over a long period of time, through the experiencing of many liturgies as well as my consequent reflections on those liturgies. As a consequence of those experiences and reflections, I was led to understand that liturgy, at its best, is musical—a product of the muses and artistry, not the product of rules or rubrics. Just as drama criticism will not create a good play, neither will "rubrics" create effective worship.

Drama School at the Catholic University of America

I was convinced that worship and theater were more closely allied than most people wanted to admit. For my own personal and professional development, I wanted the experience of learning the art of acting under competent direction. Teaching at Purcell High School I had the chance, along with Brother McQuade, S.M., to revive the school drama guild, the Queen's Men. I chose to direct a play from Shakespeare each year, while Brother chose a contemporary work. This afforded me the opportunity of working in undiluted drama and getting a feel for and a sense of fundamental theater artistry.

After seven or so years of teaching I asked Archbishop Karl J. Alter if I might study drama. He wanted me to attend Yale, "a school with a name," but I was interested in getting stage experience. I was under the illusion that stage experience was more readily and more frequently available at Catholic University of America (CUA). When the first play came around, with Helen Hayes as the star, I signed up for the tryouts. Professor Leo Brady called me aside and told me that clerics were not allowed on stage. I explained to him that getting on stage was my only reason for being at CUA, and that I had made it clear to the department head, Gilbert V. Hartke, O.P., to my faculty advisor, Donald Waters, and to everyone else who would listen that my whole purpose, my only purpose, was to get on stage and be directed as an actor. I explained that no one had said anything about a policy that discriminated against clerics. If I had been warned, I argued, when I first applied to enter the graduate program, I could have withdrawn, and I could have been off to Yale with my bishop's blessing. However, no one had given the slightest hint that onstage experience was not available to me at CUA. All my pleading and reasoning got me nowhere.

Later in the year, in a course on literary criticism, I wrote a paper on morality and aesthetics for that same Leo Brady (of *Brother Orchid* fame). Professor Brady gave me an "Excellent," and he praised my paper for a "fine and vigorous style of writing." He then opened the door to all of my pent up anger: "This is the first thing that you seemed to have your heart in!" He had not seen vigorous writing yet. I laid it all out in longhand on legal-sized tablet paper. I reviewed my reasons for being at CUA, and the reason my heart had found no home there. Further, I went on to say that a visitor to the campus, a priest of the Washington diocese, had asked me, "Is it true that you were not allowed on stage because you were Black?" I also mentioned that a fellow graduate student, Robert Murch, and I had visited a former CUA student. After introducing us, Robert said to the other young man, "Clarence has the same trouble that you had at the school." Now the man was Black, but he was not a cleric. It dawned on me that this was the very man that Fr. Hartke had bragged about as being one of the finest actors to pass through the school. Obviously, the man had been kept off stage because of his color!

I took these several pages, steeped in my anger, and had them reproduced for distribution not only to Leo Brady but also to my own bishop, the entire faculty and staff of the drama department, and a few other people that I wanted to inform. It was not until I was literally on my way home from CUA that I found out the tear that the knife of my epistle had caused in the fabric of the Drama Department. Even then, I might never have known were it not for Janet and Donald Waters; may they be forever blessed.

I bring this up in abbreviated form to say that it was the only fully deliberate obstacle placed in my way as I prepared myself to become a professional liturgist. Leo Brady and his supporters may have their counterparts ecclesiastically, but they must never be allowed to prevail. There was a great deal of good, however, that came from being at CUA. Although it was not *the* center of the American Church, it was, nonetheless, certainly *a* center for the American Church, simply because its student body and faculty/staff were drawn from every part of the country. It was also central because it was situated in the nation's capital. I was there the evening that Jimmy Hoffa came, with bodyguards and a Roman-collared chaplain, to talk to us and bragged about his ability and his intention, when it served his purpose, to shut down the country through his union. The man sent a chill through my body. Had I not been in Washington I would never have come into contact with the official and unofficial leadership of the Liturgical Conference, nor would I have been privileged to sit on its board. I might never have been invited to share my "new" music with the American Church at the meeting of the Liturgical Conference in St. Louis at Kiel Auditorium in August of 1964. The Conference convened some twenty thousand strong for the first Mass in English.

The First Mass in English

As I remember it, I was only on the program to lead one communion hymn. The song was "God Is Love" (the very first I ever composed). The music so energized the crowd, however, that I was called back, again and again, to share more of the music with the assembly. And, lucky us, the Purcell High School Mafia, (the Queen's Men, bedecked in red and scarlet blazers emblazoned with Shakespeare's coat of arms with the addition of the *fleur de lis*) was there to sell thousands of our album, *An American Mass Program.* It was not a Mass, I had insisted to Omer Westendorf, who was publishing the first "hard copies" of the music, with accompaniments by Maestro Henry Papale. (Later Henry did many arrangements of various pieces for me.) Omer liked to make or could not help making long titles: *Father Rivers Leads His Congregation in an American Mass Program.* The most I could do was get the first half of the title subordinated into small letters. Even Omer had been a bit squeamish about publishing the printed text until the money started rolling in and the "rave" reviews came in from the secular and religious presses.

At the conference in St. Louis I was made into an instant celebrity. All I did was smile and shake hands and try to answer all sorts of questions that I was ill equipped to handle. I retreated to my hotel room at night, unable to remove the frozen smile from my face and relax my aching right hand. I had learned all too quickly the price of being a celebrity, and it was not a price that I was willing to pay. The next year, I was so anxious to get away from people at the Chicago meeting of the Liturgical Conference that I exchanged my identity badge festooned with pretty ribbons for Donald Clark's plain one with only his name thereon. Shamelessly I walked the halls of the Chicago Hilton passing myself off as Donald, an almost skinny and rather tall seminarian looking nothing like me. I never dreamed that I would crave anonymity; I surprised myself.

There were three conventions the summer of 1965: Baltimore, Chicago, and Portland, Oregon. At the Portland meeting of the conference, I was invited to deliver one of the main talks, albeit in the warm-up position for Godfrey Diekmann, the star for the evening. At the Portland airport waiting for the luggage handlers to bring my bags, I was standing next to a black-suited gentleman who turned out to be Archbishop Johnson of Vancouver, British Columbia. The luggage handler took my stubs and Bishop Johnson's at the same time. I was not in clerical dress, but the gentleman (of color) who was collecting our tickets did a double take and addressed me: "Are you Father Rivers?" I nodded yes, and the man announced enthusiastically: "I'm coming to hear you tonight!" Archbishop Johnson turned and asked, "Who are you?" It was in the tone of, "Are you SOMEBODY?" I responded, "Clarence Rivers, a priest of the Cincinnati Archdiocese." Somehow that did not impress him.

At the evening of the first general assembly, with a dozen people onstage, it was my luck to be seated next to Archbishop Johnson. The experience did not seem to disturb either of us unduly. We exchanged small talk, but that question mark was still on his face. After the opening and evening prayers, I rose to address the assembly. Essentially

I gave a talk that, with humor, pointed out the faults of the American worshiping public. It was not the learned analytical talk that this crowd was used to, but they ate it up to my surprise and satisfaction. When I finished, the crowd was on its feet, cheering and applauding, as I went back to face Archbishop Johnson. The crowd would not stop, however, so I returned for a bow at least once, maybe twice. Strangely I cannot remember a thing that the eloquent Benedictine monk, Godfrey, said that night.

The Retreat for Archbishop Johnson and His Presbyterate

When we all were seated once again, the archbishop of Vancouver leaned over and whispered into my ear, "I want you to come and give a retreat for me and my clergy." I leaned back and whispered, "I'm too young." A year or so later, I received a handwritten letter from him (at my residence in the Fraternite Sacerdotale in Paris). He said that I was old enough now; he gave the dates and time, and said I should be there. It was the first and last time that I accepted an invitation to give a retreat. Not that I did not enjoy it, but I felt ill at ease giving a retreat that was full of literature, particularly poetry, to a crowd that might have been expecting something else; but I must say, they seemed to enjoy it.

The auxiliary to Archbishop Johnson was disliked by his fellow priests, and in this "crowd" of his peers he was alone and lonely. He heard what I was saying and found nothing to condemn, but he was uncomfortable with my words and somewhat in awe of this strange young priest whom he liked. With the utmost deference and politeness, he asked if I might speak to him privately. "Do you believe . . . ," and he then passed me through every article of the Apostles' Creed. This inquisition over, he said: "People like you, and with your gifts you could do a lot for the Church. Even those shoes make you likeable and attractive." He was pointing to a very comfortable pair of suede high tops, (between tan and brown) pointing out their square toes from beneath my black cassock. "All they have to know is that you are the Church's man."

The Unexpected

A Glenmary priest told me, somewhat cryptically, "They are going to give you the gold medal this year." For whatever reason I did not pay much attention to the remark, partially because the speaker gave no further details. I certainly did not know who "they" were, but sooner or later I received a letter in the style that I had come to recognize as that of Father Thomas Phelan, priest of the Albany Diocese, Newman chaplain at the Rensselaer Polytechnic Institute, and president of the *The Catholic Art Association.* I wrote back saying that certainly I would be in Houston, Texas that August to receive the award. The Art Association met in Houston a few days before the Liturgical Conference of 1966.

I do not remember how the award was presented, but it was in a plain, hand-carved, cherry wood box. The medallion itself was gleaming gold. On one side was the inscription "Recta Ratio Factibilium" (the scholastic definition of Art or Artistry: a right sense of proportion in things that can be made/done) surrounding a modified Jerusalem cross with four stars within the four equal arms of the cross. On the other side was "The Catholic Art Association," surrounding a truncated *Chi Rho,* a symbol for the name Christ, with a Greek letter in each of the symbol's five angles spelling the words "the Saviour" (Σωτηρ). The hand-lettered citation reads, in part:

> The words of the Eucharistic celebration are words of song . . .
> He has shown us the way to whole hearted song,
> in traditional Christian Worship. . . .
> His song is a genuine expression of the people of God
> on American soil.
> Houston, Texas, on the twentieth of August, anno Domini 1966
> Thomas Phelan
> President

A Change Is Called For

It had been apparent for some time that I was spreading myself too thin: teaching literature at Purcell High School; directing the Queen's Men theatre group; part-time duty in a parish (after seven years at St. Joseph's, a record for assistant pastors, I was transferred to the Church of the Assumption, in Walnut Hills); accepting invitations to do music and worship workshops on university campuses and in a few parishes; and giving lectures on race relations. Consequently, I asked Archbishop Alter to free me from regular assignments so I could concentrate on worship. He did not really understand what that meant. To help him decide, he sent (through the help of Bishop Edward McCarthy) my proposal to several liturgists, including Godfrey Diekmann, O.S.B. of Saint John's Abbey. The responses came back so positive, even enthusiastic, that the archbishop could no longer simply say "no," so we compromised. I was given my pick of liturgy schools in the United States or Europe. I first reminded him that the head of General Motors did not have to be a mechanic, but I chose to go to Paris to the Centre Pastorale de Liturgie, in the Institut Catholique.

Pere Gy, the director of the Pastoral Center, and other faculty members insisted that *"La mode ici c'est scientifique et historique!"* Everybody assumed that, beyond the class lectures, I would be pursuing a study of music, or at least a study about music. It was suggested that I contact Pere Gelineau. Father Gelineau and even the members of the faculty treated me as a peer because of my work in the United States developing a new music for worship, but I knew my limitations. I did not know anything about music from the academic perspective. I thought I might try working with a French Dominican sociologist, but he did not see any relationship between liturgy and social life.

There was a deeper problem, however: *La mode scientifique et historique*. I wanted to take another approach. Father Gy listened patiently to my exposition on liturgy and aesthetics— solving the problem of ineffective worship by examining the worship for its aesthetic effectiveness. He understood, but what I wanted was not what the school offered or should offer. We agreed to disagree. In order to get the most out of the courses without frustrating myself, I simply audited the courses so that I had a clear idea of what I could expect from an academic liturgist—or more precisely from a liturgiologist. I gave up on the idea of getting a doctorate there. It would not have proven useful, in light of my own goal. I needed to assure myself that the goal of effective worship was not just an elusive phantom, but I did receive something invaluable from the professors of the Institut Catholique. These were among the influential periti of the Vatican Council. I will relate two incidents concerning one crusty but learned member of the faculty, Dom Bernard Botte, O.S.B. All the lectures at the Institut were two hours long, with a break halfway through. My first day in class was with Dom Botte. I did not leave my place at break, and Dom Botte came straight for me. He asked, without ceremony or introduction: *"De quelle part de L'Afrique etes vous?" "Mon pere",j'ai dit, "Je ne suis pas de L'Afrique, maintenant je suis des Etats Unis!"* Immediately he lost interest; African Americans were not as exotic or as interesting to his Belgian-French mind as a native-born African. In an instant, without ceremony, he wheeled around and was back at his lecture spot, having muttered one undecipherable grunt, "Uhn!" No doubt he wanted to get firsthand knowledge of what kind of change of rites was happening in some place like the Cameroons, but I had no way of telling! Since he did not converse with me because I was not a native-born African, I thought it was funny but never took offense. Should he try that now, however, I would give him a tongue-lashing, because I am just about old enough and crusty enough to take him on—on his own terms.

Later one of the other faculty members related another Botte story. The crusty old Dom was no respecter of persons. During one session of Vatican II, a committee gathered bishops and periti together in something less than an ensemble. One extremely reactionary bishop was holding forth against a particular point that everyone else had agreed upon. When Dom Botte had his fill of the monseigneur, the crusty old Benedictine spoke up: "Monseigneur, how long have you studied or researched this matter?" "None," was the reply. "Well then," the Benedictine replied, "I've studied it for more than twenty-five years, and I think you should sit down before you embarrass yourself further."

These two instances involving Dom Bernard Botte, plus other stories told by or about other faculty gave me a human face to the Vatican Council. Some of them said that having the vernacular in each country should lead to a variety of rites. Of course, the translators—sometimes forced by bishops to be transliterators, supposedly in pursuit of orthodoxy—frequently are not true to the orthodox meaning of the texts, and certainly not true to the finest calling of their native languages. When this happens the prophesy of new language leading to new music and therefore new rites cannot possibly happen. Nor can it happen when analytical prose takes the place of poetry.

We can see, then, that the intent of the council may readily be thwarted. Living and conversing with the real fathers of the council brings and leads to understandings and reflections that council documents can never, of themselves, deliver. This shows the limits of *"La mode scientifique et historique."* Examination and analysis of documents without knowing the thinking of the writers, however thorough, may lead one terribly astray and may not be true to the documents themselves: *Ni scientifique, ni historique.*

I also learned how isolated the Atlantic Ocean can leave the Americas, and how smug and uninformed it can leave some Europeans. At a meeting of *Universa Laus* at Pamplona, Spain, the Spaniards laughed—to the point of disrespect—at the non-lisping, non-gutteral Spanish of Sergio Mendez Arceo, the bishop of Cuernavaca. This at a time when English speakers on both sides of the Atlantic had become reasonably tolerant of one another's strange handling of the language.

At that same meeting *An American Mass Program* was played; it was the only North American music that the movers and shakers in France and Germany knew of. In the summer of 1967 there was little else, and the only North American representatives there (excluding the bishop of Cuernavaca) were the newly elected Abbot Primate of the Benedictines, Rembert Weakland, O.S.B.; Clarence-Rufus J. Rivers, priest of the Cincinnati Archdiocese; and Stephen Somerville, priest of Toronto. *Universa Laus* was born in opposition to another international group that would have kept us singing mostly nineteenth-century music in Latin. Needless to say, that could not have succeeded in this country even without *Universa Laus.*

Returning to the Life of an Active Liturgist

My Relations with My Diocese: What Can We Do with Him?

I returned home from Europe mid-year of 1968. I wrote ahead informing Archbishop Alter of my plans to work full-time in the field of liturgy. Some time before, Bishop Edward McCarthy (who had been my advocate, behind the curtains, as it were) had noted that I was no longer asking permission, but rather simply informing the archbishop of my plans. I pointed out that I did "inform" well in advance and always received a response approving of my course of action. The truth is that the Archdiocese of Cincinnati did not know how to—was afraid to—make use of me and my talents in the structure of the diocese and may have been glad to be relieved of the decision.

When I was still a seminarian, as my ordination approached, the priests played the game, I think sincerely, of wondering how I might take being rejected by White parishes, and whether or not I could stand it *if* I were placed in a White parish. It never occurred to them that I might do very well in a White parish. They did assign me to teach in school that was 99.9 percent White; many were surprised that I did well there not only with the students but also with their parents. They dared not place me in a Black parish for fear of being accused of racism. I suppose the times and the prevailing "chancery" mentality did not allow them to ask me directly what I thought or desired. The seminary rector did ask me whether I wanted to be stationed in my home parish, and when I said "no," he spread it throughout the diocese that Clarence did not wish to be in a Black parish. Consequently, I was assigned to St. Joseph's, a White parish in a Black neighborhood, where the school was already significantly Black, and where the pastor, Clement J. Busemeyer, never refused any priest food and shelter, no matter who he was or what he had done.

At a later date, when my reputation was already established nationally and internationally, I turned down the advances of a Hollywood team, including an agent, a manager, and a publicist, who were in hot pursuit. Why? Because I wanted to be available in Cincinnati, if the call from the diocese should come. Of course I wanted to work in the field of worship, but I would gladly have done it for the archdiocese. The call never came, however, and I have been seeing a psychiatrist ever since. It was the severest rejection I had ever experienced—however subtle.

Please don't misunderstand me. I am supremely glad, 98.9 percent of the time, that I was left free to develop myself as a professional liturgist and to concentrate on the worship needs of the African American community. I never sought a pastorate because my experience had taught me that a pastor could not devote himself to worship. All parish priests have to compromise their pursuit of excellence in worship. That is not merely my opinion but also the opinion of those who understood and understand, and in some respects wish, that the possibilities might have been otherwise. What might have been a curse was for me, as a professional liturgist, a great grace and an undeserved blessing. Even now I shed tears once in awhile, however, not because I feel mistreated, but because I feel ignored by my own diocese.[4] In this world nothing human comes to birth without some pain. I gladly pay the price, but I am not yet a finished product! There is much yet to be learned. That is why, at age sixty-nine, I am taking voice coaching lessons. Gratefully they are paid for by the clergy's continuing education fund of the archdiocese; I could not have afforded them personally. I am also grateful that the archdiocese lets this sort of thing happen without bureaucratic red tape.

Bishop Paul F. Leibold

When I returned from Paris, for the first time since I had begun to preach effective worship, I could give myself to that task almost exclusively. I had to begin to make a living at it. I could have remained on the diocesan salary (in retrospect I should have); I could have used the income from the "road" work to maintain an office and a staff. However, I wished to blunt the criticism of those who complained to the archbishop that he was allowing me "to do as I pleased at diocesan expense." I should not have

---

4. I fear that I inherited my mother's stubborn pride. She made less money than the people she herself trained at Closson's department store, but she refused to ask for a raise, saying: "I'm not going to beg. They know my work." Neither did I think I had to ask the archdiocese for suitable work when other dioceses were expressing an interest in having me work for them. "A prophet is not without honour, save within his own country and in his own house." (Mt 7:57). On some fitting occasion, Paul Leibold quoted that to me once. He was saying this not only about me but also in reference to himself.

Clarence Rivers directs the liturgical music at a Catholic Church in the late 1960s. (Courtesy of Clarence Rivers.)

cared what they thought, since the diocese, from my perspective, had a lot to make up for in its past neglect of the Black community and its long time refusal to ordain Black priests. However, it was much more important that the Church should "hurry" to bridge the gap between itself and the Black community, and I did not have the time nor the energy to engage in petty fights. My salary was a small price to pay.

At the same time, gratefully, the administrators of the archdiocese did not see fit to pass along the petty complaints and the tattle tale reports of unappointed spies. I only knew of them indirectly from Bishop Leibold, who did not see what all the fuss was about when the right wing reported me as "being a communist sympathizer" for narrating a program sponsored by the Council of Catholic Men. Produced by the ABC television network, the writers used a book compiled by Herbert Aptheker, an acknowledged academic communist. In the book he simply reported what Blacks themselves had been saying and doing, proving that the Civil Rights movement had not just started in our times. Entitled *We Shall Be Heard,* the documentary, said Bishop Leibold, "Only told the truth."

When he later became archbishop of Cincinnati, Paul F. Leibold, in describing his role as ordinary of the archdiocese, said: "It is not my duty to run around the archdiocese putting out little fires; so please don't write me saying 'Fr. Rivers is doing this and Fr. Rivers has done that.'" He never said that to me; he did not bother me with it. He was a man of great restraint in the use of his authority. Moreover, he believed in sharing it. As a member of the first Archdiocesan Worship Commission (appointed by Archbishop Alter) I was there when Bishop Leibold declared to us all that he had only one vote. Archbishop Leibold made it clear that we did him no good service by trying to guess what he wanted and then telling him that. We had him only three years as archbishop before God called him home. In the words of an old Scottish song:"If he no e're comes this way again, we'll no e're see his likes again."

Giles Harry Pater placed a quote from Archbishop Leibold's installation sermon on his funeral program. A few days later I set it to music:

> I have come to fill my office as a witness of Christ, before all men;
> And the Christ I know from the Gospel is a meek and humble Christ
> Who came to serve and not to be served;
> And who taught by word and the example of his life
> A very simple yet most profound lesson of LOVE.

The published score was entitled "Witness of Christ." It was my first, and very minor, attempt at contemporary gospel, with the help of my longtime associate and friend, William Foster McDaniel.

My last conversation with Paul Leibold concerned dance in worship. It took place at the Jesuit Retreat House at Milford, Ohio. On one of the group walks that we took after a meal (nobody said to do it in a group or to do it at all), Paul brought up the fact that the Franciscans sprang this dance on him at an ordination in White Oak. His reaction was that it did not do much to inspire him—just a bunch of wiggling down the aisle. I knew exactly what he meant. I would have hated it. I have never allowed it in a liturgy that I controlled, but I could not pass up the temptation of teasing him. I said, "There is the old adage about casting pearls before swine." He responded typically: "You may be right."

> Sleep in peace Paul Leibold!
> *In pace in idipsum, dormiam et requiescam*
> *At the very heart of peace, I shall sleep and I shall rest.*
> Sleep in peace! We shall no e'er see your likes again!

Universities and Parishes, but Beginning at Grailville

Grailville, Ohio was the place I escaped to, and on occasion the Ladies of the Grail and I collaborated in readings and liturgies. On the rarest of occasions, we slaughtered T. S. Elliot's *Murder in the Cathedral* in a former horse barn called the Caravansery. One summer I was slaughtered as the only actor in the film *Newborn Again,* scripted by Elaine Jones and filmed, produced, and directed by the "slave driver," Maclovia Rodriguez. It was all good experience in the process of developing this self-styled liturgist. It was at Grailville, in a wonderful barn later refurbished into an oratory, that I recorded

An American Mass Program with the help of the Queen's Men and members of the Grail, and with Mary Kane out-singing us all. It was there, at Grailville, that I held an Extended Workshop on the Performing Arts in Worship with Purcell students and at least one out-of-town seminarian. He was an outstanding young man, an organist, who was sent all the way from Menlo Park, California by his seminary rector (come to think of it, this rector was extraordinary). I do not remember who else there was—perhaps a priest or two.

All of this leads up to a very ordinary happening at Grailville that begot extraordinary results. One day the Reverend Dr. James Stewart Leslie, chaplain at Ohio Wesleyan University, was visiting Grailville and heard me cantoring and leading a congregation in singing "God Is Love." He liked what he heard and invited me to Delaware, Ohio and the campus of Ohio Wesleyan University. If memory serves—leaving out details—I worked with the chapel choir and prepared a program for the student body (chapels were still obligatory on Methodist-supported campuses). The students liked the results, and James became my agent (foregoing the usual 10 percent cut), securing invitations for me at one Wesleyan University campus after another and even an invitation to one Baptist campus (Kalamazoo College, I believe). At the chaplain's home church, I learned that not every Baptist was on fire with congregational singing. I had already discovered that at the local Presbyterian church in Delaware, Ohio through the Jim Leslie connection. It was there that I jested with the pastor, "I thought that all Protestant congregations sang. " Quick with wit and tongue, he retorted, "And you eat nothing but fried chicken and watermelon?"

At the beginning of my life on the road, Protestant and Catholic university chaplains were the main sponsors of our programs. They were mainly interested in the "new" music, but the experience that came packaged for them was much more worship oriented than some might have expected. In fact, I was wary of the response that some might have had about my music: "Well, it is nice, but it might seem out of place in worship." Therefore, I seldom presented it outside of some kind of worship setting. As we shifted from college scenes to parish-based programs, we moved more precisely into an emphasis on "effective worship." The one element that remained constant, however, was our insistence on *active* participation by people attending our workshops, for active participation was the only way that people got the heart of our message. Indeed, the medium was the message. Onlookers are outsiders who rarely, if ever, experience the same phenomenon as the participants. Edmund Carpenter, an anthropologist and author of *Oh What Blow That Phantom Gave Me,* spoke about this as a weakness in the work of his peers. He gave as an example the work of an anthropologist studying Eskimo initiation rites. Such a scientist, sitting beyond the outer circle of the initiation ceremony, observes objectively, scientifically (meaning emotional non-evolvement), notating in minute detail everything that happens. The presumption is that factual (visual) detail is all that matters, all that happens, and the full truth. Wrong! The tragedy, says Dr. Carpenter, is that, many generations later, some descendant of the original group will presume to restore his "lost" heritage by enacting the notated details found in the "scientist's" book, but the result is shallow and hollow.

I am reminded of a visit that we, the Martin Luther King Fellows—Black church scholars—and I, had with a back-to-African-roots group. This group of city dwellers, with the sincerest of intentions, had replanted themselves in a South Carolina woods so infested with mosquitoes that they literally made a mask on the face of the Chief, with whom we were trying to hold a conversation. No sensible native African would have put up with that mosquito distraction for a moment. But this honest and righteous man, in the name of African heritage, would not even fan the mosquitoes away. God bless him!

The Transition from Traveling Dog and Pony Shows to Stationary Ones

Many Black parishes, indeed most Black parishes, were not being reached for several reasons. Their pastors thought that our workshops were too expensive, and they never managed to realize they might even make a profit by heading a program, based in their parishes, for the whole diocese. I found out late in the game that each parish wanted its "own" program and would never consider collaboration. Some thought their parishioners simply were not "ready"; if so, then the basic reasons were Black self-hatred mightily buttressed by some form of racism. Some thought that hiring a Black musician not connected with the traditional Black churches was the answer they sought, but in this latter case they acquired a narrow focus of Black music with no governing principles of liturgy.

Mr. Joseph Dulin, president of the Black Catholic Lay Caucus, thought he could shame me into coming for free; but I was not Cardinal John Dearden. He did not know me or understand that good liturgy did not come from heaven free of charge. There were many Black parishes that did invite us. I am eternally grateful to them and their pastors, for they gave me as much as I gave them. Henry Offer, pastor of St. Francis Xavier's Church in Baltimore, called for our services when few others might have and was most cooperative. Because it proved to be good for his people and for their *esprit de corps,* we were invited back a second year. His church attendance increased twofold to threefold.

The First National Workshop: The University of Detroit

As the summer of 1971 approached, Joseph Dulin encouraged the Black Clergy Caucus and the Black Sisters Conference to meet with the Black Catholic Lay Caucus in Detroit. This gave me an idea: why not have—under sponsorship of the National Office For Black Catholics (NOBC), Brother Joseph Davis, S.M., executive director— a workshop in liturgy and music for Black Catholics before the Lay Caucus meeting. The workshop could then supply the music and worship for the meeting in Detroit. With the help of Sr. Mary Ann Smith, who did outstanding administrative, organizational, and public relations leg work in Detroit, and with the cooperation of Garland Jaggers, from Cardinal Dearden's offices, the program turned out fine. Brother Davis sent Michael St. Julien from the staff of the NOBC to help. Mr. Redmond from the University of Detroit staff saw to it that we lacked nothing the university could offer.

I had made a special trip to Detroit to meet with Mr. Dulin and his board. I had asked specifically if what I was proposing, in light of Mr. Dulin's invitation, would be in line with what the Lay Caucus and their president had in mind. The answer was a positive "yes!" I returned to Cincinnati with the full cooperation of the NOBC and, I thought, the approval of Mr. Dulin and his board. David Camele developed the national mailing pieces and posters for the event. The latter were to be sent to Sr. Mary Ann Smith for distribution in Detroit.

Before we could go to press, however, the connection with the Lay Caucus, which had pleaded for a show of unity and solidarity, had proved to be no proof against the "Amos and Andy lodge meeting" politics of Mr. Dulin's Lay Caucus Board. We could not have the closing concert of the workshop open the caucus meeting, and, believe it or not, the reason given was that they were gathering to do serious business, not to be entertained! We changed the posters before they went to press. Then, by the time of the workshop's opening, we were no longer supplying the liturgies for the caucus, and a youth choir from Baltimore was supplying the music! I will not here go into the petty jealousies and myopic small mindedness, which my mother classified as "n——r s—-t." Strangely, none of this bothered me; perhaps, as my mother had characterized it, I simply did not want to play in the dirt lest I besoiled myself. More to the point, Sr. Mary Ann Smith made it possible for us to carry on with the workshop as if nothing had happened. Cincinnati and Dayton, with the no-nonsense persistence of Mattie Davis and a little prodding from me in the Cincinnati area, allowed us to send two Greyhound buses full of participants from the Archdiocese of Cincinnati.

Participants came from Connecticut, New York, New Jersey, Ohio, Pennsylvania, Kentucky, Michigan, Illinois, Maryland, Oklahoma, and Minnesota. It was apparent that the way to reach widespread numbers of Black Catholics was to invite them to a central location. Unfortunately, these individuals could not take the workshop experiences home except in their own somewhat changed (converted?) persons. They were professional singers with careers and just plain teenagers that the late Mattie Davis (a woman of grand spiritual dimensions and great determination) rounded up from Dayton, Ohio.

The participants worked hard during the day and entertained themselves and each other in the evenings with dancing, arias from operas, pop music of the day, and their own compositions. Joyce Jaxon, who was there, later became music supervisor for the Detroit school system. Marjorie Burrow was then a teenager who later became a leading influence in compiling and shaping *Lead Me, Guide Me*, the Black Catholic hymnal. The late Keith Davis, an unimaginable high school baritone, went on to Broadway.

In addition to my daily lectures and discussions on worship, there were daily music sessions. The faculty members for these sessions were chosen to teach a wide variety of musics: gospel, spirituals, renaissance, baroque, and my own "new" music. Edwin R. Hawkins (who brought his whole family with him: Walter, Trumaine, Daniel, and Lynette) taught his contemporary gospel sound fresh from the pop charts. Mc-Kinley Genwright taught spirituals, renaissance, and baroque pieces. William Foster McDaniel, music director for the Fantastiks, brought the feel of jazz in his piano accompaniment and fresh jazz improvisations. Along with these music professionals, I was there with my satchel of tricks.

The workshop climaxed with a two-and-a-half-hour concert before an enthusiastic, packed house. The purely musical results were spotty at best, but the spirit of the event was pure magic. We made a two-record album culled from the many pieces in the program. CBS producers Joe Clement and Bernie Seabrooks video-taped the whole concert, and made a half-hour documentary of the event. They had come to cover the meeting of the Catholic Lay Caucus but found it to be reminiscent of certain "lodge" meetings. In spite of my own immediate reactions and in defense of Mr. Dulin and the Lay Caucus, I must say that "all people find self-government a difficult process." Witness the more than two hundred-year history of the United States Congress! The Lay Caucus, so recently born, was just approaching the toddler stage.

Looking back at "Freeing the Spirit," the name I had given to all my workshops, the event in Detroit was, in one respect, a coming of age event for Stimuli (the incorporation under which I worked) and the NOBC. The work I had been doing in my own name was now, in this instance and for the first time, a work of the National Office For Black Catholics. Soon afterwards, I became, under the administration of Joe Davis, S.M., the first director of Culture and Worship, with due acknowledgement of the paving work done by Michael Mtumishi St. Julien. Up until this event, the focus of the NOBC was to educate the White clergy and religious who staffed most Black parishes.

Joseph Morgan Davis of the Society of Mary, Cincinnati Province

A word must be inserted here about the leadership of Joe Davis. The Black Catholic movement of the mid-twentieth century was just finding its walking legs. There was an element of our group and a side of many of us that found it easier to "fight" than to build. This element of us found it much easier to make demands of the American hierarchy and to yell at the bishops across a conference table. Do not mistake me—some yelling and name calling was justified. However, the wiser, saner heads knew that when the vituperation was over, the pieces of our dreams had to be picked up from the litter-strewn floor and reconstructed.

I learned a bit about Joseph Morgan Davis from the man he fought with in public and compromised with in private, Bishop Joseph Bernardin (not a cardinal until Chicago). In a lose-lose situation for the Black Catholics and the American hierarchy, Joseph L. Bernardin and Joseph M. Davis met in private and came up with a solution that overcame the logjam that was created at the conference table by intransigent bishops and uncompromising representatives of the Black Catholic community.

Before there was an official, professional connection between the NOBC and myself, Joseph Morgan Davis asked me to come to Washington to talk to Bernardin

*Brother Joe Davis, S.M.,
first executive director of the
National Office for Black
Catholics. (Courtesy of Fr.
James Pawlicki, S.V.D.,
Bay St. Louis, Mississippi,
photographer.)*

about a eucharistic prayer (by Grayson Warren Brown) that had appeared in the new journal *Freeing the Spirit*. Some members of the American hierarchy wanted to withdraw the funding for the NOBC for this transgression against "authorized" prayers (some Protestant and Jewish scholars wondered how prayers could be authorized). It took no time at all for Bishop Bernardin and me to reach an agreement that said the prayer was not necessarily recommended. It was given as an example of what a prayer might look like if it reflected current concerns in the African American community. Oh, the triumphs of ecclesial diplomacy! That afternoon in Washington was the first time I had met Joseph Louis Bernardin, and I mean no disrespect when I call him "the Diplomat without Peer."

When the Cincinnati Black Catholic Caucus wanted to integrate into Archbishop Bernardin's bureaucracy, he called a public meeting for us to air the question. When most people had spoken, I rose to express my opposition to the idea. After all other reasons had been compiled, it remained clear that our independent executive secretary would become an employee of the "White" archbishop. Archbishop Bernardin agreed with me and said publicly: "If your organization becomes a part of my bureaucracy, you will lose much more than you will gain. Your organization will become mine." Reason did not prevail, however, and fear of losing funding carried the day.

Joe Davis, Dave Camele, and CJ Rivers: Not Quite the Trinity but Close

Back to the main story—Stimuli and the NOBC, myself, and Joseph Morgan Davis. My office remained in Cincinnati, and Joseph predicted it would outlive the NOBC. I say that only because it demonstrated his respect for me and my work, which made it much simpler for us to work together. One of my first assignments was to put together the public relations package in preparation for the NOBC's first national fund raising campaign. After I had all the words that Joseph wanted to include—i.e., "Concerned Black Catholics,"—in the official name of the project, I was free to use my own judgment as to what and how much or how little to say. The matter was simple; I added my pearls of wisdom and passed them on to my collaborator in design, David Gabriel Camele, whom every Black Catholic, outside of Cincinnati, presumed to be Black. It was a firm belief among Selma natives like my mother that Italians were other than White: "She said she married a White man, but he was a 'Dago.'" My own reactions were that "When Hannibal crossed the Alps and descended on Italy, he left more than elephant s— behind." But in all seriousness, the mentality of the designer himself and the quality of his art were far more important than his race or ethnic origins. After forty years of collaboration, it is difficult for David and me to know who taught whom what. For 99 percent of my work he is the designer of choice. When he asks what is the other 1 percent, I reply my living room and my bedroom. If you are puzzled, so is he.

The next venture of note that I directed for the NOBC was the second Workshop in Liturgy and Music. Still riding on the warm air currents of the Detroit workshop, concert, and CBS documentary, I felt that going to Catholic New Orleans would bring even greater returns—not financial but evangelical—in spreading the gospel, the glad tidings, and the good news of Freeing the Spirit. Unfortunately, I was wrong! The great White Father and designated spokesperson for the Black Catholic community commented that the workshop budget was larger than his school's budget. I felt grateful that I was not associated with his school. I returned to Cincinnati and raised money from my fellow priests who would not profit even indirectly from the program. One of the first things I heard upon arriving in New Orleans was that people in the diocesan offices had taken offense at an image printed on the exterior envelope of the public relations package—the silhouette of a young Black man singing. The problem was Black self-hatred, especially among some of those who called themselves Creoles. (As if we all were not Creoles. In the original usage of the word only Native Americans were not Creole.) Unfortunately, this self-hatred (linked partially to skin tone) was reinforced by the Church establishment working in the Black community. Had it not been for the energetic, enthusiastic work of Michael Mtumishi St. Julien, the program would have had much less success than it did. Some time later Aline St. Julien wrote a scathing denunciation of this Church that drove her own children away.[5]

---

5. Aline St. Julien, "Holy Mother the Church . . . An Unfit Mother," *Freeing the Spirit* 3 (1974): 4–9.

Even without the help of the establishment, we had a full turnout of people from all over the country, including a reasonable number of very talented people from New Orleans, not all of whom were Catholic. Edwin Hawkins came back, without his retinue, having asked that Brother Joe Davis not be allowed to talk so long. Bishop Perry showed up for the concert and brought Archbishop Hallinan with him. Thanks to the public relations efforts of Michael (Aline's son), a local disc jockey broadcast the concert, and the good news was spread even farther and deeper in and around New Orleans than we had hoped for. Some who had not wanted to be associated with us before we started were present by the end of the concert. The smug and arrogant director of the program took great delight in not accepting invitations to cocktails afterwards. Under the circumstances, it felt good being petty, though I knew I was reacting in anger and that I was wrong in doing so.

The Ordination of Bishop Joseph Lawson Howze: Jackson, Mississippi

When the Diocese of Jackson announced that Joseph Lawson Howze would be ordained bishop, Brother Joe Davis, director of the NOBC, saw the event as a major happening for the Church in the Black community. After all, it was only the second ordination of a person of color since the ordination of Bishop Harold Perry, and it was the first ordination of a Black bishop to which the now organized Black Catholics might contribute. It was with this in mind that he called Bishop Joseph B. Brunini and his vicar general, Monsignor Bernard Law, who had somehow arranged to have me invited to participate in the preparation for the ordination.

In practice it meant that I would be the music director for the ordination, since there was very little influence we could bring to bear on the shape of the liturgy itself. That was all right, because in directing the element of music we could create and shape the spirit of the whole event. I went to Jackson, Mississippi and got to know Msgr. Law through long conversations. I thought we were well on the way to becoming very good friends. About Bishop Brunini, the ordinary of Jackson, it must be said that he was a man of the earth, literally, tending his garden and being as hospitable to the stranger as the proverbial desert nomad. One had to like him; I found it inconceivable that anyone would not like him. I had never before met a bishop like him.

At any rate, Msgr. Law said that Bishop Howze had only one musical request: "The Church's One Foundation," sung to the tune called "Aurelia." Either it was already in the program I had designed, or I found a place to insert it. I submitted the entire program to Msgr. Law for his review, and we were on our way. The cathedral music director, who was a very competent musician and a pleasure to work with, told me, with regret in his voice, that most of the cathedral choir declined to sing with us. The few that did were worth their weight in gold, and the ones who could not overcome their racial prejudices gave us not a curse but a blessing. The blessing came in the form of enthusiastic singers from Meridian, Mississippi, who were glad to make the trip every evening and sing their hearts out. Other singers came from Jackson State, along with a wonderful brass section that made the Ralph Vaughn Williams arrangement of "Old One Hundreth" easily solemn and a joy to sing. It did not sound as good at the coronation of Elizabeth II of the House of Windsor. One cannot say too much in praise of the volunteers who drove nightly from Meridian for rehearsals; nor, indeed, could one say too much in grateful praise of the young Black instrumentalists and singers from Jackson State, who added glory and grace to the celebration in Jackson's Civic Auditorium (the cathedral was far too small). The pianist for the occasion was a young man from Jackson by the name of Donald Thigpen. It was the first time he worked with me but not the last. I remember that the name of the hymn tune was "Aurelia," because the lady who organized the Jackson State participation was named Aurelia. Golden she was!

Black Catholics gathered in significant numbers from all over the country, and the Jackson Civic Auditorium was filled to capacity. Before the solemn celebration could begin, as was my practice, I climbed up on my perch (some wag might call it a crow's nest) rigged for the occasion and made sure that everyone knew the music and would sing it lustily, making a joy-filled, heavenly noise. The congregation responded as the occasion warranted. During the ordination itself, Bishop Brunini's smile beamed all over the gathering. He looked every bit the benign and generous *paterfamilias* that he was. After the newly ordained bishop had been presented to the assembly, the choir took up the song that I had composed in memory of Archbishop Leibold "Witness of Christ." The ordaining papal nuncio, impatient to be on time for his flight back to Washington, ordered the music to be cut short, but the blessed son of Ireland (may his tribe increase) who was the master of ceremonies somehow did not get to me in time. He had stopped backstage to make sure that his shoes were still polished.

When the last lingering note of the recessional was still in the air, I saw from my perch a man making his way through the crowd from the far end of the auditorium. Somehow I knew he was aiming for me. I was thinking, "What did I do now?" Remember, we were in Mississippi; it simply never occurred to me that we had done something right, very right. When he arrived, he introduced himself as Lieutenant Governor Winters. I had read the name in some news magazine. I felt flattered. Mississippi indeed, where the cathedral choir (most of them) would not sing with us. I really missed them.

To backtrack, I was not long into the preparation for Bishop Howze's ordination when the idea occurred to me that the NOBC ought to make a significant symbolic gift to Bishops Howze and Perry. I explained my idea to Dave Camele: superimpose my Black spirit on a square cross in red, black, and green enamel. The NOBC Board was still very pedestrian, so I undertook the expense myself. David designed not only crosses but boxes to house them, made symbolically of several African hard woods and American black walnut. The results were stunning, and I spent a better part of my last three days before the ordination putting a hard paste-wax shine on the boxes. I wrapped the finished product in motel towels (it was raining) and ran over to the cathedral rectory where a reception was being held. It never occurred to me that I might look out of place in my denim jeans and Chuck Taylor Converse sneakers; it was my usual dress. I walked through the front door of the rectory, and on my way to the back room I was stopped three times and asked very politely by people I did not know (it was not my first time in the rectory), "May I help you?" The first time I said, "No thank you," not giving it a second thought. By the second and third time, I began to catch on. I played innocent and reached the back room where I met the bishops and Joe Davis. I managed to deliver the crosses to Brother Davis, pass pleasant banter with people I knew, and have a snack or two before I decided to get back to my hermitage at the motel, where I could cause less chaos. By the time I started to leave, however, word had spread about that little Black man in sneakers. The Black gentleman who had offered to help me on my way in now begged my pardon on my way out. I am slow, but I have been Black since I can remember being anything and quickly translated "Can I help you?" into "You don't belong here!" Having made the translation, I had continued on my errand with a certain smugness that I am capable of when I know "they" are in the wrong. I do not think I am capable of real malice, but there is something of "Puck" in me.

David made those first crosses by hand out of zinc. Since then I have managed to get others stamped out of silver or other metal and then gold plated. Regrettably I have not managed to keep them available for subsequent bishops. The cost is prohibitive, and there was never any guarantee that they would be sought for newly ordained bishops. When he was ordained, Bishop Edward K. Braxton wanted one, but there was no way I could have one made. I bring the matter up for two reasons: the leadership in the Black Catholic community can be just as blind sacramentally as any of their fellow Catholics and place little value, if any, on signs and symbols, and no individual without substantial means can shoulder the cost of such a tradition. No matter that the imagination for religious/cultural development is available; it is for naught, if the means are not available.

The Books and the Doctorate

Soulfull Worship

At some point near the beginning of our "official" working together, Joseph Davis asked if I would publish some of the liturgies that I had put together. I convinced him that this would be futile if one expected the *"esprit"* of the original liturgies to be lifted off the printed page. We made the effort, however, and reinforced the attempt with a prelude of several essays. The text of each service was accompanied by notes explaining why we did what we did. The result was the first of two volumes on worship, entitled *Soulfull Worship*. (The *full* of *Soulfull* is intentional, *soulful* has different overtones).

I had given up on the idea of acquiring a doctorate. The experiences of friends who had taken the traditional route to the Ph.D. convinced me, if I needed convincing, that I did not need useless suffering for the sake of additional letters behind my name. If the relatively benign process of the Pastoral Center in Paris was not suitable for my purposes, what would be? Meanwhile I went about my research into the worship of the traditional Black church—looking for the connection between the worship of traditional religions in West Africa and the worship of the Black church (regardless of denominational names). I knew that the music of the Black church was *sui generis* and had too much internal strength to be merely a derivative (not to mention a distortion) of European music. It was most likely that Black religion was not a derivative of colonial religion. Rather, Blacks looked at the scriptures with totally different eyes and heard different messages; their religion emphasized themes that the colonials were not about to preach to an enslaved population. Contemporary attitudes toward religion in the Black church, in some respects, are distinctly different from that in the White church. In the common parlance, "church" sometimes has a distinctly derogatory connotation (boring and dead come to mind) in the White community, but "to have church" in the Black community connotes excitement and "a good time."

I was writing and reflecting on these matters, thinking of the process already begun by some of borrowing indiscriminately certain externals from the Black church in order to breathe life into the worship of the Black Catholic community. How were we to do this without being caught in the trap of mere mimicry of Black church practices? The latter attempt has all of the pitfalls of "reconstructing initiation rites from the detailed notes of an 'observant' anthropologist." This did not mean that we should discard and dismiss observable practices from the traditional Black church; it is a caution against slavish mimicry.

The Reverend Doctor Henry Heywood Mitchell and the Martin Luther King Scholars

While pursuing and verifying observations from the traditional Black church, I contacted notable members of that church, seeking input from them for the magazine *Freeing the Spirit*. I was particularly eager to speak with Dr. Henry Mitchell. It was around this time that Dr. Mitchell was putting together a program with a twofold goal: (1) getting material about the Black church gathered by the men and women who had been most successful in that church; and (2) to reward them with doctor of ministry degrees for their groundbreaking efforts. About the second year of the program I was invited on board as a consultant and to give Black Catholics some representation in a heavily Baptist group.

When I arrived in Atlanta in the summer of 1973 for the second session of the Martin Luther King Fellows[6] (the first session having been held the previous summer in Ghana and Nigeria), I found a community of people who began each day with worship and then spent the best hours of the day sharing one another's insights,

---

6. For a fuller treatment of the MLK Fellows, see *Freeing the Spirit* 2, nos. 3 and 4.

experiences, and research on/in the Black church. Each day one or two of the fellows presented a paper or the outline of a paper that the rest of the participants (faculty, consultants, and fellows) evaluated first for technical precision and later for content. The group helped the individual shape his or her paper both for consistency of logic and the accuracy of the subject matter. Here was the first time, in my experience, that doctoral candidates and faculty advisors worked together for a significant time, instead of working almost totally in isolation. This alone was stimulating, but even more stimulating was the fact that they were doing what no one else had done before—putting down on paper an analysis of the Black church experience.

Afro-American culture-religion cannot really be understood without understanding its basis in our original African cultures. For that reason, I will always treasure an experience that my participation in the MLK Fellows afforded in the summer of 1973. We visited the Sea Islands off the coast of Charleston, South Carolina. In a little church one evening, amid the polyrhythms of hands and feet, sounding as authentic as a chorus of Africa drums could sound, undergirding the soulful chanting of "I heard the voice of Jesus say: Come unto me and rest," I truly *experienced* the continuity of African culture in America. What I had previously known cerebrally[7] now became basic knowledge. I have wished in vain to share that kind of understanding, that "moment of enlightenment"; like a private revelation, it is impossible to share it fully. One can only talk about it, and that is very inadequate. I might add at this point that I had to be converted (self-converted) to the possibility of the continuity of African culture in the Americas. When my friend Boniface Luykx first brought up the notion, I almost laughed in his face (but I did not). I denied the possibility, since I had not consciously experienced it. As I have said before, I may be slow getting out of the gate, but it did not take long for a full conversion to take place. All I had to do was open my eyes and ears.

African American Religion in Jamaica

In the winter of that year, January 1974, the MLK Fellows visited Jamaica and Haiti for a firsthand experience of the African American religions in the Caribbean. In Jamaica we had three very wonderful guides. Ms. Olive Lewin spoke to us about music in Jamaica. Mr. Edward Seaga had an intimate knowledge of little-known religions like Pocomania; he himself had lived among the Pocomania people and had become a Pocomania shepherd. Dr. Rex Nettleford was a philosopher and original thinker who had an enlightening "world view" on the necessary moral impact of African culture throughout the Americas and, indeed, worldwide. He issued a word of caution: African Americans must be free to define themselves, but they must be careful so as not to define themselves outside the human race. The experiences and the lectures were heady stuff, but the best was yet to come, in Haiti.

---

7. See "The Continuity of African Culture in the Diaspora," a paper I wrote with the sponsorship of the Rockefeller Foundation.

A Side Bar

I met a gentleman in downtown Kingston, and we engaged in conversation over Cokes. I asked him where everyone went at night; downtown was empty! He said they met in one another's homes, and that some families were in the habit of charging a few cents each to people who wanted to gather in a decently commodious space to dance. I said I wanted to see it all; I did. The reason for this digression is that when we visited the home of a friend of his, he introduced me by my name, Clarence Rivers. When the man who was inviting us in heard the name, his eyes got as big as saucers. Before we could clear the door, he reached behind himself and pulled out a record, and holding it up he asked, "This Clarence Rivers?" *An American Mass Program* had traveled. This is an indication of the cultural vacuum that existed in the Church at that time. Indeed, that cultural vacuum had been fostered by Church "authorities" and the church's music establishment. I am reminded of the supper we shared at Archbishop Emmanuel Milingo's residence in Lusaka, Zambia. He insisted that we should sing with him a song from the charismatic movement in the United States. He intoned my "Bless the Lord" ("Glory to God, Glory"). We "sang" through it, to his beaming delight; he had brought something new to J. J. Braun (then provincial of the "White Fathers") and myself. He did not have a clue that he was singing my song (badly, like the charismatics). I decided I did not want to enlighten him. Why, with such a rich musical culture indigenous to his people, would he pick up a song sung in such a third-rate manner and bring it back to Lusaka like a shiny new treasure? Because the "missionaries" had brought with them the same oppressive attitudes about church music that had stifled the development of church music all over Europe and America. When this same archbishop dared to have healing services like American charismatics but with indigenous props and dress, the Vatican bureaucracy snatched him off his throne and had him examined for insanity. An outrage!

African American Religion in Haiti: Voodoo

Meanwhile back in the Caribbean, I told our guide and Voodoo scholar, Michel Laguerre, that Gertrude Morris wanted me to bring her a Voodoo doll. He had incredulity written all over his face; I knew I had blundered. He had never heard of a Voodoo doll. I should have known better; I did know better, but. . . . Voodoo dolls are just one of those gross distortions that abound about Voodoo. Dr. Laguerre, a Jesuit, was finishing his doctorate at the University of Illinois. He had been born in a little Haitian village on the Dominican Republic border. Besides having known Voodoo from the inside, he had made Voodoo his main academic study.

I had suggested that Michel Laguerre would be the best possible guide in Haiti because he spoke Creole, French, and English; besides, he had been breathing Voodoo air since his birth. He proved far more impressive than I had imagined, and I knew of his scholarship. In his lectures he held the MLK Fellows spellbound (not too strong a word), and he did it through what I considered a very heavy French/Creole accent. The fellows were willing to listen much more closely than they otherwise might have

Vol. III, No. 1: 1974
THE MAGAZINE OF BLACK LITURGY PUBLISHED BY THE NATIONAL OFFICE FOR BLACK CATHOLICS

Freeing
the Spirit

This cover of Freeing the Spirit *depicts an article on Voodoo written by Clarence Rivers. The journal was edited by Clarence Rivers and published by the National Office for Black Catholics. (Courtesy: Clarence Rivers.)*

because they were captivated by his subject matter. They were equally captivated by his scholarship and his unflinching objectivity in his criticism of the Catholic Church. I do not think these Black church ministers were used to such objectivity in their own environs. They were impressed, but the best was yet to come. He arranged for us to be present at an authentic Voodoo service.

In the Voodoo service there was one moment of very slight embarrassment, but it was offset by an extended period of exhilarating exaltation and pure ecstasy. The chief priest had given us a tour of his "inner sanctum," where most people are never allowed. I suppose he thought we were not likely to steal any of his "power" by seeing his objects of "magic" that he kept there, including votive lights, a small, fading, painted plaster statue of Jesus, the Sacred Heart of Jesus, a cross or two, and other objects such as herbs and potions in vases and jars.

During the service, when he was demonstrating his access to spiritual power, he came around to me and baring his chest he said, *"Couper moi!"* Well, I was not going to cut him even with Michel whispering loudly, "Cut him." It took a moment or two for both Michel and I to realize that in French and Creole the word *"couper"* means both to cut and to strike. All I had to do was give him a little blow no stronger than a *mea culpa* strike to one's own chest. In my irrational moments I like to think that he came to me because he was told that I was a Catholic priest, and he knew, therefore, that I had power to spare. Next time I will cooperate more readily, but I will also need to be informed ahead of time. That was a slight embarrassment, not nearly as humiliating as a couple of *faux pas* I fell into, such as trying to speak French in Paris.

Back to the service, the main effort was to evoke possession by the spirit or spirits of God, and the main evocation was through chanting and dancing to the rhythms of sacred drums. There was a whole line of priestesses dressed in white who danced fairly simply but continuously once they started; they were led by a tall, very lithe priest. His steps became increasingly complex, along with his handling of a ceremonial sword or knife. He left me breathless. It was one of the few times that I have been uplifted by a dance. I had dreams of bringing him home or sending for him to demonstrate the power and potential of a religious dance. I have seen nothing like it, before or after. I do not even remember a single distinct movement, yet I am breathless with the vague remembrance of the event that took place almost thirty years ago.

Nothing that I have mentioned captures the essence of that service. The next morning I laid my thoughts open to the scrutiny of the assembled Black church ministers and the MLK Fellows. "What I experienced last night was the same thing that I have experienced in traditional Black church services." No one denied it. There were grunts of agreement, and the one or two that did articulate in sentences agreed. It is a striking instance of not being able to judge a religious experience by a catalog of all the externals. Now I had my "missing" link that connected West African religions, the traditional Black church, and the African American religions of the Caribbean. It also links these religions with biblical religion, not with the religion of the Temple as we know it, but with the religion of the minor prophets and the New Testament. Why else is Pentecost, the Christian feast of the Holy Spirit, considered the birthday of the Church, when, in fact, Christianity as we know it did not begin to manifest itself for another sixty or seventy years? I believe because it is the day of empowerment by the Spirit that we consider *the* birthday of the Church.

When we were in Haiti, Archbishop Ligonde, the bishop of Port-au-Prince, and I had a long private conversation. Among other things we discussed was the fact that the local churches in other cultures could not become authentic as long as they were dominated by Europeans and European Americans. I hear him now in his exact words: "There can be no Catholicism in Haiti apart from Voodoo." He could never say that aloud without either going into schism or submitting to an humiliating experience from the Vatican, such as what happened to the former bishop of Lusaka, Archbishop Milingo.

This brings me back to Voodoo. Most Voodoo churches in Haiti require that their congregants be baptized Catholics; Episcopalians are acceptable and Protestants as well, if there is no way around it. This is not merely my facetious wit at work. The

Protestant missionaries were late on the scene in Haiti, coming after most of the Voodoo culture had crystallized. The Voodooist sees no contradiction between Christianity and Voodooism. Why, then, is there no traditional Black church in Haiti? It is fairly simple. In Haiti, unlike in the Protestant United States, access to the priesthood is denied to Blacks by the hierarchical Catholic Church. Therefore, an indigenous Catholic/Christian Church is impossible. There were no indigenous clergy to establish their own syncretism of Christianity with African culture in the pattern of the U.S. Black church. Contrary to common belief, the traditional Black church is not essentially the result of a White missionary effort. Even so, Christianity and Voodoo would have merged visibly from the beginning in Haiti. Thus, it is not altogether surprising to find so many Catholic externals in Voodoo.

The International Eucharistic Congress

The International Eucharistic Congress was held in Philadelphia the summer of 1976, the year of the American bicentennial. The powers that be in Philadelphia appointed one of their own, Mr. Bob James, to chair a national committee to launch and oversee the Black Heritage program. For whatever reason, I was not appointed to the committee. I knew it would be a mess, and, out of a sincere concern for the reputation (not nationally but internationally) of the Black Catholic community, I thought I had better intervene. I wanted to do so without getting tangled up in the ecclesial intrigues of Cardinal John Krol's deputies, both high and low, however, so I wrote a two-page proposal of the background and outline of a program. I called Bob James, read the two pages to him, and said that I would mail them to him. He asked me to come to the committee meeting and make the presentation: "They would accept the ideas, if you presented them." "But I'm not a member of the committee," I said, trying to make a point. He said that was not a problem and missed the point. I went and bit my tongue at the suggestion of a candlelight procession through the streets ending at the Spectrum for Mass. The people who supported this idea had no inkling of the logistical nightmare it would be to get several thousand people into position to march (process?). You just cannot have a procession of thousands of people and end up with an orderly—forget inspiring—Mass. When everybody was finished, or even before that, I said I had a suggestion. Copies of my proposal were passed out. I explained it, and I think the vote to accept passed unanimously. Brother Joseph Hager was appointed executive director. We had a conversation or two, but Joseph was competent. That satisfied me. If he needed me he would call. Approximately a year later, I got a call from Bob James, who wanted me to take over as executive director. A friend of mine had been appointed director by Bob James, and I had no intention of undermining Joseph. I do not remember how many times Robert called and I said "no." Finally Monsignor Conway called: "Come to Philadelphia. We need you; you know nobody can bring this off except you." Meanwhile I was thinking, "There are only six or fewer months left. Why are you asking me now?" I did not voice any of that, however. I really did not want to get involved, but, to play for time while I notified Joseph, I said that I would think it over.

I called Joseph immediately: "Joseph, they're trying to give your job away. Moreover, they're trying to give it to me. I'm not going to accept it." Joe replied, "Look Clarence, I'm asking you to take the job." He explained that he and the diocesan staff came to an impasse over the budget; all communications had broken down, and they had not spoken for months. At Joe's request—and against my better judgment—I said I would take over the program, but I was determined to have no interference from people who presumed to speak for the cardinal. Remember what Archbishop Leibold said to a group of his advisors: "If you try to guess what I think and then try to tell me that, you do me no good." I think a lot of "no good" presumptions were entrenched in and out of Cardinal Krol's staff, and these "no good" presumptions were sometimes acted on without consulting the cardinal. They did him and the community "no good."

I asked Bob James why they were asking me to take over now. I have only his word for it, but at least a part of his response seems credible. At a Board of Governors meeting for the congress, there were reports from the various committees that had programs for the congress, but there was none from the Black Heritage Committee. When the cardinal asked about the Black Heritage Committee's report, Msgr. Conway somehow explained that the committee was not functioning and had no report, but he read the two-page proposal that I had submitted. They thought that sounded fine, and asked who wrote it. Msgr. Conway replied, "Fr. Rivers." "What part does Father Rivers have in implementing this program?" asked the cardinal. This is where my disbelief kicks in. When told I had no part in implementing the program, the cardinal said, "Well, if Father Rivers has no part in implementing the program, we won't fund it." It is possible, even likely, that they said get the "little s—" involved, swallowing hard as they said it.[8] Even then I doubt very much that anyone said, "If not, there will be no funding." I think that is a line that Bob used to massage my ego. Unlike people with a small sense of self, my ego is vigorous and does not need massaging. Before saying an absolute "yes," I wrote out my conditions for Msgr. Conway. I received a nonspecific *carte blanche* in response, but I chose to interpret it as agreement to my conditions. If any interference came from the diocesan bureaucracy, I intended, with politeness and firmness, to hold them to the fullest meaning of *carte blanche*.

Why was I acting so hard-nosed? I did not trust the bureaucracy that stood between me and the Philadelphia hierarchy. Remember the "no good" policy that the archbishop of Cincinnati had to denounce. If it could happen there, it could certainly happen in Philadelphia.

Once I was reasonably assured that Msgr. Conway would be a man of his word, Dave Camele and I went to Philadelphia and met with a few people. David measured

---

8. It was not the first time I had been "not wanted" in Philadelphia and yet was begged to come. I have the impression there may have even been groans, internally of course. The complaint of Henry II about Becket might have been more apt: "Will no one rid us of this meddlesome priest?" Only I wasn't meddlesome, except for writing that two pages of "helpful" notes. In retrospect that was meddlesome.

the Spectrum almost minutely. Within two weeks we had finished all the plans, including a seating plan; a design for the altar platform; a design for vestments and all the other paraphernalia (banners, processional cross, etc.); commitments from speakers, ghost writers (yes, a dozen of them), and other participants; commitments from music directors, singers, and instrumentalists; and commissioned music arrangements. In one day I had raised (with about a dozen phone calls) the ten thousand dollars needed for the new vestments we had designed.

When we got back to the Board of Governors so soon with detailed drawings, they were amazed. My budget was approved, and Msgr. Conway, true to his word, did not allow his financial crew to mess with it. It included a trip to several places in Africa to meet with committed speakers and Cardinal Maurice Otunga, archbishop of Nairobi, who was to preside at the liturgy. The bureaucrats did not see the need for that: "We've invited Mother Teresa, and nobody has to go and talk with her." I tried to explain that my speakers had to cover relatively new ground in politically alien territory. Msgr. Conway simply dismissed the bureaucrats from the room, assured that I thought the expense was necessary. When they were gone, we talked about other things, and he gave me his personal assurance that if any of his people got in the way, he would take care of it. I should come straight to him. With that, David and I were off to New York to a textile wholesaler, where we bought bolts and bolts of material in red, black, and green. (By the way, Sears used the same material for golf pants.)

Afterward I went home and had major surgery; my throat was cut to remove a few overactive parathyroid glands. Some think that the surgeon did not cut nearly enough. (Will no man rid us of this meddlesome priest!?!) I was in intensive care for four days, back in my room for two days, and in two weeks off to Africa with my surgeon's blessing. It was my first trip to the Mother Continent, and it was exhilarating. I spent a week or so in Kumasi with Bishop Sarpong. I met Professor Kofi Asare Opoku at the University of Ghana and had supper with him and his family. For dessert he went out to the garden and cut a ripe pineapple; I enjoyed a fresh pineapple for the first and only time in my life. I met dozens of bishops; I was making courtesy calls to assure them of paid expenses for the congress. Everyone was hospitable and courteous, with one exception: the cardinal archbishop of Dakar, Hyacinthe Thiandioum and his Irish nun-secretary, who within sight and hearing of the cardinal (reading his breviary) said he was busy and could not see me. It was the only act of discourtesy I found on the continent in twenty years of occasional travel there.

Without appointment, I called at Cardinal Otunga's residence, and his Irish priest-secretary invited me to come right over. We spent several hours telling one another our stories about being Black in the Catholic Church. When he returned to Nairobi after becoming a cardinal, the so-called missionaries tied a black dog in red ribbons and threw it in his yard. There was very little that I had to tell him that he had not experienced. I warned him that we might have trouble getting an appropriate eucharistic prayer approved for the congress. He was ready.

Like the first visit to anywhere, the trip to Mother Africa was stimulating; but that is not always good. At the hotel I met Peter Jennings. "Are you a British actor?" I asked.

When he finally stopped laughing, I asked why he was not behind the anchor desk at ABC. He was covering the hijacking of the airliner carrying Jews to Israel. No wonder Entebbe airport was dark. Thank God it was not dawn when we left Entebbe for Nairobi, because the Israeli commandos might have shot first and asked questions about that burning Ethiopian Airlines plane much too late. That was close and much too stimulating. (Who was to know that in a dozen or so years later I would meet in Zambia a young man named Bruno, a political refugee from Idi Amin's days, and bring him to the United States. My son is now a naturalized citizen and doing well. After all, he comes from a long line of East African merchants. Buying and selling is in his blood.)

Back home I was receiving the prayers and sermon I had commissioned from the MLK scholars and, most importantly, the music compositions and arrangements from Maestro Henry Papale. I simply had to have the music printed in a single booklet to send to the music directors. The eucharistic prayer, translated into Black prayer style, had to be digested and rewritten into a coherent pattern in the Western Church tradition. Several liturgists said that it was the best they had seen at that time. Still, I knew we would have trouble.[9] I asked Archbishop Bernardin to use every avenue possible to get the eucharistic prayer authorized. (If one of our fellow priests were to preside, I would not have asked for authorization, but we had Cardinal Otunga presiding. I could not embarrass him.) When the prayer was not approved, I became angry at Bernardin, because I thought he had not really tried hard enough.

I returned to Philadelphia three weeks before the congress. On the way back I had stopped off in Washington to meet with Bishop Eugene A. Marino, who was to preach a ghostwritten sermon. None of the sermons suited him. I said I would take one and rewrite it. I took outright accusations against Church authorities for neglecting its pastoral role to be catholic, universal, and open to the culture of all people, specifically to the culture of African Americans, and turned them into statements that Bishop Marino would be comfortable in saying. Basically, I wrote that the Church knew there was much in each area that still needed to be done, and Bishop Marino added quotes from Church documents that supported the need for action in those areas.

Once I was back in Philadelphia I made sure that everything was in place. I wanted to be certain that Father David Benz, a Black priest of the Philadelphia Archdiocese and a very fine administrator, knew all he needed to know to take over from me. I notified Msgr. Conway and company that all was in order and I was returning home. I explained that I could not in good conscience preside over a program that simply included a few Black-flavored songs as the only contribution of African Americans to the prayer life of the Church in front of an international congregation. I promised to go away quietly, leaving a full program in place and all my people in charge, insuring as good a program as there could be under the circumstances.

---

9. As president of the Bishops' Conference, Archbishop Bernardin, then archbishop of Cincinnati, had to be invited to the opening but was not invited to the entire congress. He and Cardinal Krol had had a disagreement.

It was not my intention to do so, but this move brought out the big guns, including an auxiliary bishop of the archdiocese. They implored me to stay, saying they would do whatever it would take to get the eucharistic prayer authorized. If necessary, they would go to Rome. Frankly, I do not think they fully comprehended that my work was done. The program, under the competent administration of David Benz, was not about to fall apart. Against my better judgment, but wanting to believe they would do what they promised, I said I would stay. They had promised a great deal; God knows how great the good might be if they brought it off. They were going to New York to meet the pope's personal representative at the congress, Cardinal Knox, prefect of the congregation that controlled matters liturgical. I said I would like to meet him and present my own case. They said they would present whatever case I prepared, so I put it in their hands and proceeded to forget about it, trusting soul that I am.

We were two or three days into our program of speakers, including Bishop Sarpong and Professor Opoku (both from Ghana), Dr. Henry Mitchell, and a young priest fresh from Louvain with doctorates in philosophy and theology, Edward Kenneth Braxton (now Bishop of Lake Charles). Everything was going well. The speakers were good, and people were enjoying the presentations. David and Mary Ellen Camele were there to take care of last minute arrangements. It was as if we were in the garden of Eden! But I forgot about the damned serpent.

On the day before the climactic liturgy, Msgr. McManus from White Plains, New York, contacted me to tell me that I had been lied to. My presentation package was on his desk as I had "sealed" it. My blood pressure went through the ceiling. I tried to get a press conference, but the public relations office declined to get me one. I was the only person they had speak to the press for the last three weeks. Now I had to find "neutral" ground? That proved impossible, so I left the last minute attempts to produce something good in the hands of Joe Davis and Jim Lyke. They had taken the case to Cardinal Otunga, who was on his way to take the case to Cardinal Knox, whose secretary he had been. Then in walks Mr. Big, Bob James, who could not even find us a set of timpani in all of Philadelphia and who had begged me to take this job in the first place: "I'm the head of the Black Heritage Committee, and I know Cardinal Krol doesn't want anyone bothering Cardinal Knox." This wee man had cut Cardinal Maurice Otunga's diplomatic legs out from under him. Gratefully, I was not told about this until much later.

You reap what you sow, however. Even though I never had the chance to call a press conference, the public relations office distributed a paper defending the Philadelphia hierarchy against what they thought I might say, so the national press came looking for me. Since I had not seen what had been distributed to the press, I did not know what they were talking about until one of them asked what I had against the Mass prayers. I answered without so much as a nanosecond of thought: "The prayers of the Roman Sacramentary, especially in the English translation, are bland, insipid, and tasteless. The African American prayer tradition that we might have used is so much more dynamic and is aesthetically superior. " Next morning's headlines read "Black Priest Says

Mass Prayers Bland, Insipid, and Tasteless." That was not the last word from me or from the media, however; gratefully, there was a Black journalist there by the name of Chuck Stone. That impromptu press conference was followed by the Mass, which substantially overshadowed all the dirt and anger that preceded it. The music, much of it arranged by Maestro Henry Papale and some of it composed for the occasion by him, was under the capable direction of Avon Evans Gillespie. Ronald Dean Harbor was at the piano, and there was an organ combining with the sound of a drumming group in consort with a timpanist for the processional, "Black Thankfulness." [10] Chuck Stone, the Black journalist and syndicated columnist, who was present and caught the spirit of the evening, wrote of it quite tellingly.

"Mass for Blacks: 'Man, We Had Church'"

Only the Heavenly Father could have pulled it off. . . . What we did, children, was to carry on, praying, singing and clapping our hands in a giant fiesta of happiness. . . . We "had Church" . . . created by Clarence Rivers, a priest from Cincinnati. Into his inspired service, this liturgical genius, this choreographer for the Lord, wove together the divine threads of Catholic prayers, African drumming, and black American Gospel music.

Even the colors emancipated tradition. All the black bishops . . . wore the international black liberation colors of red, black, and green. . . . Bishop Eugene A. Marino . . . explained the reason in his homily . . . : "When . . . Pope Paul [VI] visited the Martyr's shrine in Uganda, he raised up the possibility . . . of . . . a glorious dream . . . that black people might enrich the Church with their unique and treasured gift of negritude . . ."

Last night that dream lofted into partial fulfillment. . . . "The drums have called us to worship," exclaimed Dr. Avon Gillespie, a college professor of music. . . "Let the people say 'Amen'!" . . . the congregation swung into . . . "Spirit of Life." I walked over to Father Rivers and hugged him, "Clarence, we're having Church. . . . "

Arthur Patterson, a cornstalk skinny . . . waiter from Cincinnati . . . r'ared back, closed his eyes and cradled the Spectrum with a soul drenching joy . . . in the [song] "When From Our Exile." In one line, the words were written to be sung "we'll think we're dreaming." He sang it, "we'll think . . . we'll think . . . " then reached somewhere in the rafters and shouted "Lord," held the note and kept on soaring up to another "we'll think."

---

10. The drummers and the timpanist were brought all the way from Cincinnati, because Mr. James could not find a drumming group in all of Philadelphia, nor, indeed, a set of timpani. Sr. Francesca Thompson, on the other hand, who did not live in Philadelphia, found us a set of timpani in only a few minutes. I am still in shock at the thought of a man who begged me to take a job, then contributed nothing to the program, and in one stroke sabotaged it and embarrassed an African cardinal who was trying to be an ally.

In a gesture that betokened my gratitude, I met Cardinal Otunga for dinner in New York before he returned to Nairobi and presented him with a gift of the miter and stole from the new set of vestments made for the congress. Subsequently, he came to see me at the Sisters of Mercy Hospital in Nairobi where I stayed overnight fighting some intestinal infection picked up in my sojourns on the continent in 1980 or 1982 with John Joe Brawn, then provincial of the "White Fathers."

It was too much. Many stood and waved their hands in the black church tradition when the Spirit has moved you.

The only Nun onstage, Sister Francesca Thompson, stood in moving jubilation, proof that negritude never slumbers. . . . Kenya's Maurice Cardinal Otunga's impassive ebony face never betrayed any emotion . . . this dignified shepherd remained the Church disciplinarian.

"Its not what we wanted it to be," declared a tired but triumphant Father Rivers to the congregation, "but it was more than many might have expected."

For that spiritual gladness let the world shout a loud and glorious "Amen." [11]

The Doctorate: Union Graduate School

Work with the Martin Luther King Fellows restored my faith in the possibility of a doctoral program that could meet my needs. A friend persuaded me to contact Dr. Roy Fairfield, a professor at Antioch College and co-founder of the Union Graduate School (UGS), then headquartered in Yellow Springs, Ohio (now the Union Institute is headquartered in Cincinnati). Dr. Fairfield was quite persuasive. Had he tried to persuade directly, I would have been very wary, but he did not. In fact, he had no way of knowing that I might need persuading. He described the Union's "way" to the doctorate for "self-motivated learners" and similar eccentrics. I was, to say the least, impressed. It was what I needed in order to complete my work on the synthesis between African (African American) culture/religion and European American worship forms/styles. There was no place on this planet where the subject was approached, and it certainly was not taught. There was no expert on the subject that I could name. Only the Union would give me full rein to continue pursuing the subject on my own. The Union process for the doctoral candidate worked as follows: (1) set up an academic committee of roughly five persons (more adjunct faculty can be chosen if the help is needed and the student can afford them and their transportation back and forth); (2) choose a core faculty person from the Union faculty; (3) choose a committee of two chief faculty advisors in your particular field; and (4) choose two peers—candidates going through the process or who have completed their work and been graduated within five years past.

For my core faculty person I chose Professor Edward C. Wingard, Ph.D., dean of the Education Department at Central State University. He could get me through the Union process correctly and on time. I liked his cool style—strong and sure of himself, with no personality hangups to get snared on. I really did not need an advisor who was not self-assured and whose hand had to be held. In our first conversation, after having heard him present himself at the first colloquium that I attended, he proved beyond a doubt that I had chosen well. He was good for me; he was not intimidated by me or my subject, was a great advisor on the ins and outs of the process, and had no idolatrous in-

---

11. *Philadelphia Daily News,* 5 August 1976.

*Sr. Francesca Thompson, O.S.F.,
keynote speaker at the Black Catholic
Congress, 1988. (Courtesy of Fr.
James Pawlicki, S.V.D., Bay St. Louis,
Mississippi, photographer.)*

clinations toward the Union process itself. A person who worships anything other than the "Unknown and Unknowable God, The Ultimate Foundation of the Universe" could have you making very strange and unnecessary pilgrimages. With Dr. Wingard nothing was sacred except the Sacred.

There was no one on the Union faculty who was familiar with my field of research/work, so I chose a long time friend and collaborator, now professor of drama at Marian College in Indianapolis, Sr. Francesca Thompson, O.S.F. (Oldenburg) as one of the my chief faculty advisors. She had done her doctoral work in theatre at the University of Michigan and was told that she would never find enough material to research the Lafayette Players, the first Black theatre company in New York. Her mother and father were members of that troupe; her mother was a (perhaps *the*) major star of the company. It was hard work but she proved the academic skeptics wrong and unearthed an old treasure that has yet to be fully viewed. Since the Aristotelian principles (with a grain of salt) of theatre were at the heart of my approach, I needed a drama expert, and Francesca Thompson, Ph.D. was my choice. I did not know of anyone available to me, and perhaps available anywhere, who had as much expertise. Since I was playing to a Church crowd, Father Eugene H. Maly, doctor of sacred theology and, more importantly, doctor of sacred scripture, was my other choice for adjunct professor. I had notions about spirit possession that needed to be exhibited in light of the Biblical parallels. I had known Gene since I was in grade school, when he was freshly ordained, residing in the parish of Saints Edward and Ann while learning Middle Eastern languages at the Hebrew Union College. There was no better scholar anywhere.

With the help of Dr. Wingard, I chose the Reverend Dr. Richard Righter, a Presbyterian minister from Dayton already through the process, and Joyce Quinlan, still in the process, as my peer advisors. An additional peer was Sister Marilyn, a nun in the Episcopal Church. I also kept Dr. Roy Fairfield within reaching distance, in case of problems. He would be quite helpful when the staff of UGS and I disagreed on any point, and I wanted to argue from the perspective of "the mind of the founders."

One met with one's academic committee as often as was necessary to get the job done. The absolute minimum would have been an initial meeting to get one's proposed work (content and process) approved and a final meeting to approve of the completed work. I had two or three more meetings than that, plus consultations in person and by phone with individuals. I kept Dr. Wingard busy with my affairs and made occasional calls to Dr. Fairfield. Outside the group meetings, I only met once with Gene Maly, to be sure that my notions about the "orthodoxy" spirit possession in Voodoo and the traditional Black church was in line with spirit possession in the Bible. That was relatively simple, but Rev. Dr. Eugene Maly wanted to wander with me in an area that might be identified as the "chicken and egg syndrome." I had made a strong declaration for the case that "ortho-praxis" had to precede "ortho-doxy." Eugene was something of a Platonist and thought that all the right ideas had to preexist their incarnate forms. He was partly right but did not fully understand that there would be no critics, unless there were playwrights and theatres producing their works. As I said, it was the chicken and egg syndrome. We dwelt on the subject at length. As he rightly perceived, an essential part of my work took for granted that incarnate truth is more reliable than dogma-based activity.

There was very little new writing that I had to do in this process, but I did need more experience of the worship in the traditional Black church. First I concentrated on getting more of that experience by worshiping in those churches as a member of the congregation. Only after I had completed that did I turn to ordering my thoughts in writing for my PDE, i.e., Project Demonstrating Excellence, which in its final form was a book complementing *Soulfull Worship* entitled *The Spirit in Worship.* Rightly understood, both volumes had the same name. When I had finished writing, I submitted the book to the scrutiny of my committee and other concerned people.

For financial and other reasons, my goal was to finish my work at the UGS in one year, understanding that twenty or more years had been spent getting to that point. The flexibility of the UGS process allowed for those considerations, though in most cases their concern in those days was to limit the maximum number of years (seven) in the process.

Long time friends of mine and long time patrons of Stimuli, Gerald David and Jeanne Etienne Rape, would not hear of a graduation that was less than public. They went about acquiring the facilities of Mt. St. Mary's Seminary in Norwood: the faculty dining room for my academic committee to dine in before its final meeting upstairs; the chapel for the actual graduation ceremony; the Aula Magna (the great hall) for the reception; and, not the least, the caterers that ran the seminary dining facilities to supply the grand supper for my committee and thousands of hors d'oeuvres and drinks for the "public."

I entered the Union Graduate School on 27 March 1977, and I was graduated on 27 March 1978. As Jeanne and Jerry had determined, it was a public (anyone was welcome) ceremony with a nice-sized crowd (one hundred to two hundred persons), mainly people I knew personally or professionally. The procession included the Archbishop of Cincinnati, Joseph Louis Bernardin, draped in renaissance finery—a Feraiolo (the rose side of purple) over black cassock with a rose sash and buttons—as I had requested; many of the seminary faculty in their doctoral gowns with various hoods; my academic committee appropriately gowned; and myself in a new black mohair and wool blend suit. Under the direction of Ronald Dean Harbor, the organ with timpani, choir, and congregation greeted us with my favorite processional, "Old One Hundreth," as arranged by Ralph Vaughn Williams for the coronation of Elizabeth II. Oh, I do love pageantry!

I began by introducing my academic committee. I said that I had chosen them for their due subservience to me and my cause. That did it. They roasted me—such tongues! Ed Wingard announced that true to my nature I had demanded his attention almost any time I felt the need, presuming to interrupt his work at Central State or intruding on his time with his wife and family in Xenia, Ohio. Father Maly started by saying that he had known me for some forty years, and by this time he would have expected some change for the better. He finally admitted that I had lived up to his expectations. I do not remember everything that everybody said in the roast that I had incited unintentionally, but each ended with a formula: "And for these reasons I add my name to this diploma, in the name of the Union Graduate School." Each, in due turn, signed the diploma, hand-lettered on real sheepskin in less than two weeks. The UGS office would take six weeks to get a machine-printed copy, but I was glad that Dr. Fairfield recommended making a diploma specific to my discipline. Without it we would not have had that wonderful signing ceremony, in public, with each member of the academic committee signing his or her own name—with a fountain pen, not a ballpoint.

When all the signing was finished and they had dressed me in gown and hood, Archbishop Bernardin went out of his way to explain that I already had the right to wear the stole from ordination.[12] Only then, as was his appointed task, he went on to present me

---

12. I never figured out what diplomatic ploy he was engaging in. The people present could not have cared less. To this day I wish he had joined in the "roast." He is the only prelate that I grabbed by the lapels. Lord knows that I meant him no disrespect. I was trying to drag him away from his young secretary so that whatever angry word I might utter would have been heard only by him. I told him that I had never asked anything for myself but always for the Black Catholic community, and that in no case had he ever been able to deliver. I am sure he understood my frustration. But we remained friends, I hope. When he was leaving Cincinnati, I got the usual calls from the national and local press. I said that he had an understanding that no other White bishop had; I had tried on many occasions to personally teach him a few things, and he was

with a stole to match the academic gown: light blue on dark blue outlined by an over-lay of gold threads in a pattern of flowing waters.

Marcus Prensky, a friend that I had met in Paris and a virtuoso on the guitar and the lute, brought his lute and serenaded the assembly with two renaissance pieces:

> Start the Music,
> Strike the Drums,
> Sound the song-full Strings.
> (Ps 81:3)

With African drumming and classical organ plus choir, the ceremony lofted to a close to the strains of "Black Thankfulness":

> Halleluia, Halleluia, Halleluia! Amen!
> Thank the Lord for the Holy Spirit,
> Who revives my soul again!

The ceremony had a blend of cultural elements! Side by side there was solemnity with humour, and all of it with grace and style. To say that I was pleased does not come near to what I actually felt.

A Liturgical Conversion

At some point in the late 1970s or early 1980s, I had an inclination of thought that hardened into a conviction: weekend workshops or extended workshops in worship might leave people renewed and refreshed spiritually, or even give them a grasp of in-tellectual abstractions about the ingredients of effective worship, but nothing short of an unlimited *apprenticeship* in the art of structuring and building *effective worship* will guarantee us an effective means of handing on that artistry and insure the making of professionals in worship. These professionals will in turn be our guarantee that there will be, as long as it is required, bright beacons of effective worship burning in our darkness.

At first I had the idea of taking over some abandoned inner city parish as the locus of this training, the gathering place of this college. It was only after I was frustrated in the pursuit of such a parish church, with rectory and convent as residences, that I could hear clearly what another voice, namely, that of my friend and associate, David Camele, had been saying. Rectories and convents would not be suitable dwellings for

---

always receptive. In our last conversation, he thanked me for being nice to him in the media. I said, "I only spoke the truth." My bishops have always conversed freely with me, and, I think, with most other members of their presbyteriate. That is just the Cincinnati way.

full-time resident staff and apprentices. He was quite correct. Now I am looking for an appropriate site to build. We would need apartments, not monk's cells. In addition, there has to be an administrative building with classrooms, gathering halls, and dining facilities. We would need a church building seating at least five hundred, with ample space for an uncrowded altar and pulpit, appropriate aisles for processions, special sound and lighting facilities, and other spaces and qualities.

Like most teenagers, I feel eternal at my age (sixty-nine approaching seventy), but I need to consider the *remote possibility* that I may not be around to bring this dream to a beginning, not to mention a conclusion. Should I not be preparing others to take over this work? Though I do not want to think of such a thing, nonetheless, I must. Otherwise the dream may die with the dreamer. What I have envisioned is a complex idea and process, not easily reduced to words, but I will try as soon as it is financially feasible to bring together a number of people who can, over the period of several summers, *experience* as well as *hear articulated* what it is that I have in mind—the process and the product. If they can buy into the dream, they will become members of the *Lion of Judah Covenant*; then they along with me, or (God help us) without me, will build and run the *Lion of Judah Institute*, a program in which liturgical apprentices will become liturgical professionals.

The Lion Of Judah Institute

a college of apprenticeship
to graduate not only scholars,
but especially worship professionals,
liturgical practitioners, worship impresarios

An apprenticeship program is necessary because we are dealing in matters of aesthetics. Matters/principles of *taste and prudent pastoral judgment cannot be handed on in a rule book,* at least not yet, and maybe never. They can be absorbed over a period of time, however, from intimate involvement in appropriate liturgical and other aesthetic experiences. This is the usual way any art or craft is learned. Our professionals must become liturgical impresarios, having at ready command the skills and sense of artistry, *mutatis mutandis,* that a producer-director-playwright should have. Additionally, each should be a liturgical master of ceremonies, rooted in his or her religious tradition.

We would be willing to take into this program persons of different religious traditions and *both men and women.* Although the program was conceived to train persons working in Black Catholic circumstances, *the principles learned would be applicable to other circumstances and traditions,* including both ritual and nonritual traditions. We will be able to mold worship professionals of any faith. Certainly we could help the various Black church traditions so they might pass without trauma from a rural-based worship into whatever they may develop. Moreover, we would be of great service to various European traditions, in the New World or east of the Atlantic, by sharing broadly the gift of negritude as Paul VI exhorted us to do.

Beginning with human religious needs and the responses that can be found for them in the *Poetics* of Aristotle (not being fundamentalists, however, in interpreting Aristotle), our graduates will be able to guarantee a well-constructed and effective service, hopefully in the bounds set by each religious tradition. We are especially concerned to share our ability to focus, as through a light-bending lens, the drama of worship so that it may be a point of spiritual warmth and vitality, activating the assembly and moving and inspiring those assembled to continued growth, conversion, healing, and, indeed, to transcendence. We are as certain as humans can be, after years of observation, experience, and study, that *"we know how to deliver the goods."*

Since no such program has ever existed, it can only happen among people and through people who are not afraid of thinking big. The present ordinary, Archbishop Daniel Edward Pilarczyk, once asked me, "Can't you do anything that isn't grand?" I replied, "I can, of course, think small (I do so grocery shopping, house cleaning, etc.), but not when I am seeking something grand! And, I'll admit, too grand for me. But it is not my grandeur I seek but the grandeur of the Kingdom of God." After his second inaugural address, in which he laid a basis of a reconstructed Union of the States, Abraham Lincoln asked Frederick Douglass, "What did you think of the speech?" Douglass replied, "Mr. President, it was a sacred effort." In the borrowed words of several spirituals and the Book of Revelation, I am making a sacred effort. For I am seeking a place of beauty and bright mansions—a place with no want, no pain, no tears. It begins in the Sacred Liturgy of our churches around "The Sacred Table of the Lord":

j

I am seeking for a city, Halleluia!

For a City in that Kingdom, Halleluia

j

And I saw the Holy City

New Jerusalem

Behold the dwelling place

Of God with Man-Kind

j

And the material of its wall was jasper

But the City itself was pure gold

And the foundation of the City's wall

Was adorned with every precious stone

j

The first foundation Jasper

The second Sapphire

The third Agate

The Eighth Beryl, the ninth Topaz

The twelfth Amethyst

j

And the twelve gates were twelve pearls

And the streets of the city were pure gold

j

The City has no need of Sun nor Moon

For the glory of God is its light

And nations shall walk by the light thereof

j

I am seeking for a City, Halleluia!!!

For a City in that Kingdom, Halleluia!

And I don't feel no ways tired!

Oh, Glory Halleluia!

j

Deus in adjutorium meum intende!

Domine, ad adjuvandum me Festina!

Festina!

j

Enlighten Us All!

For where there is no light, no prophetic vision

Surely people will perish!

j

Clarence-Rufus J. Rivers, Ph.D., Cincinnati, Ohio, February 14, Anno Domini 2001

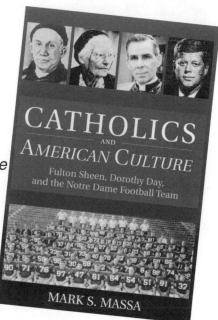

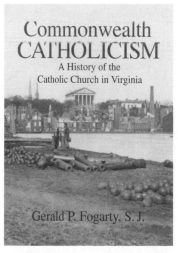

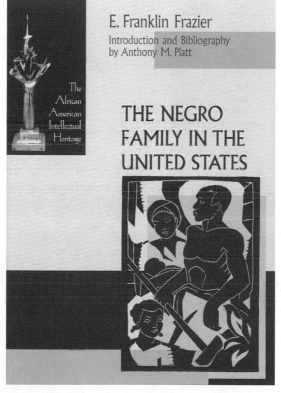

The African American Intellectual Heritage Series

WHAT THE NEGRO WANTS

RAYFORD W. LOGAN

Introduction by Kenneth Robert Janken

Review of 1944 edition:

". . . a book of true importance."
—*Chicago Sun-Times*

Written by fifteen promi-nent African American intellectuals, including Langston Hughes, Ster-ling Brown, and W. E. B. Du Bois, *What the Negro Wants* helped set the agenda for the Civil Rights Movement. This edition includes a new introduction and an updated bibliography.

0-268-01966-5
$36.95 cl
0-268-01964-9
$22.95 pa
416 pages

Rayford W. Logan
New Introduction by
Kenneth Robert Janken

The African American Intellectual Heritage

WHAT THE NEGRO WANTS

WITH ESSAYS BY:

RAYFORD W. LOGAN
W. E. BURGHARDT DU BOIS
LESLIE PINCKNEY HILL
CHARLES H. WESLEY
ROY WILKINS
A. PHILIP RANDOLPH
WILLARD S. TOWNSEND
DOXEY A. WILKERSON
GORDON B. HANCOCK
MARY McLEOD BETHUNE
FREDERICK D. PATTERSON
GEORGE S. SCHUYLER
LANGSTON HUGHES
STERLING A. BROWN